A. E. King

3 Jan 1995

ROBERT L. MILLETT

CHRIST-CENTERED LIVING

BOOKCRAFT
Salt Lake City, Utah

Library of Congress Catalog Card Number: 94-71750
ISBN 0-88494-934-6

First Printing, 1994

Printed in the United States of America

To Shauna,
whose silent sermons have taught me
so very much about Christ-centered living

And we talk of Christ,
we rejoice in Christ,
we preach of Christ,
we prophesy of Christ, . . .
that our children may know
to what source they may look
for a remission of their sins.

—2 Nephi 25:26

Contents

Preface

Jesus Christ is the Light of the world. By him we are enabled to see all things. Through him and by means of his redeeming power, we are able to accomplish what would otherwise be the impossible. In him is to be found the peace and tranquility that the world so desperately seeks. Without him there would be no hope for joy and happiness here or eternal life and exaltation hereafter.

Truly, Jesus of Nazareth is the central figure in all of human history. We measure time according to his birth, truth according to his teachings, and goodness according to his impeccable and matchless mortal life. Because of him, the erring and straying soul may be reclaimed. Because of him, those who have been beaten and scarred by the pain and irony of this existence may be healed and soothed. Because of him, death has no sting and the grave has no victory. With Nephi of old, we glory in truth, we glory in plainness, and we glory in our Jesus, for he has redeemed our souls from hell (see 2 Nephi 33:6). This book is an effort to glory in the goodness, power, mercy, and grace of the Holy Messiah. It seeks to focus on the manner in which light and life and love flow into the lives of those who come to trust in and rely upon him who is the Author of the abundant life.

In the preparation of this book I owe a special debt of gratitude to Lori Soza, my capable and conscientious secretary and assistant; to James Christensen, Greg Olsen, and Gary Smith for allowing us to incorporate their artwork in this volume; to the staff and management of Bookcraft Publishers, including Russell Orton, Cory Maxwell, and Jana Erickson for their willingness to attempt something a bit unusual, and to my dear and trusted friend George Bickerstaff for his careful and inspired editorial eye. Although in what I have written I have sincerely sought to be in harmony with the sermons and writings of prophets both ancient and modern, this project is not an official publication of either The Church of Jesus Christ of Latter-day Saints or Brigham Young University. Though I owe so very much to so many, I alone am responsible for the conclusions drawn from the evidence cited.

I concur with the timeless adage that that man or woman is most truly successful whose life most closely parallels the life of the Master. Our Lord and Savior is the Way, the Truth, and the Life (see John 14:6). In a world where false Christs—meaning false systems of salvation—shout for our attention and proselyte for our involvement, the lowly Nazarene stands at the door of the human heart and knocks softly. He beckons. He invites. He offers not only to forgive our sins and to raise us from death but also to make us into people with purpose, to transform us into men and women who know who they are and whose they are. Christ-centered living is the object and design of those who call themselves Christians, those who look to Jesus in every thought, who call upon him in triumph as well as in tragedy, who yearn to embody righteousness and truth. The path to life and light is strait and narrow, but the Keeper of the Gate is ever ready to succor the weak, to lift up the hands that hang down, and to strengthen the feeble knees. He waits at the end of that path, not alone to certify us, but also to welcome us.

The Christocentricity of Mormonism

In recent years the criticism of Mormons and their exclusion from the category of *Christian* have intensified. There are those who feel uncomfortable with us because we believe in modern prophets and in scripture additional to the Bible. Others reject our testimony of Jesus because we believe that men and women can become like God. Many shun the Latter-day Saints because we do not subscribe to the creeds of Christendom. Whatever the cause, it has become fashionable in modern religious circles to assign to Mormons the derisive label of *cult* and to exclude us from current conversations simply because we are not, by their reckoning, Christian.

Mormons have had more than their share of ironic abuse on this matter of being called Christian. On what basis do we claim to be Christian? We believe in Jesus

Christ. We believe he is the Son of the Eternal Father, the Only Begotten in the flesh. We acknowledge him as Lord and Savior, as Redeemer and God. We take his name, apply his blood, and seek to emulate his life. We know there is no happiness or joy, no lasting peace or contentment, independent of the new life produced by the transforming powers of Jesus Christ. We teach and we testify that there is no salvation, no exaltation, no eternal life, no hope of eternal glory, no reconciliation with the Father except by and through the man that was and is God—even Jesus of Nazareth. The irony, of course, in all the exclusionary criticism is that Jesus Christ is the heart and core of our faith, and the Restoration is indeed the restoration of his gospel, his Church, and his ordinances. That way of life, that system of salvation and Eternalism which we have come to affectionately know as Mormonism, is Christ-centered and Christ-directed. We are his servants, and he is our Lord and Master.

Joseph Smith and the Revelation of Christ

Joseph Smith's introduction to Jesus Christ came in the Sacred Grove in the spring of 1820. There was reaffirmed in that monumental theophany the fundamental Christian teaching—that Jesus of Nazareth lived, died, was buried, and rose from the tomb into glorious immortality. In the midst of that light that shone above the brightness of the sun stood the resurrected Lord Jesus in company with his Father, the Almighty Elohim. Joseph Smith knew from the time of the First Vision that death was not the end, that life continues after one's physical demise, that another realm of existence—a postmortal sphere—does in fact exist. Through open vision, by visitations, and by voice Joseph Smith came to know his Lord as few men have ever known him. The revelations that came through Joseph Smith made the latter-day seer acquainted with the mind and voice and will of the Master. Joseph came to know first-hand how to commune with Jehovah.

Like Jesus, the Prophet Joseph Smith was called upon to endure a special kind of loneliness. His was not only a life characterized by persecution and suspicion but also an isolated existence known only to those who walk in the glorious light of the noonday sun, who themselves know with an absolute certainty and yet must minister among others who seem to walk and talk in the dusk, those who struggle with faith, those who doubt, and even those who dare not believe. The farm boy who grew to become a prophet's prophet could bear a personal witness of his divine Redeemer, for Joseph was also, to some degree at least, a man of sorrows and acquainted with grief, one who knew directly the costs of Christian discipleship. "God is my friend," he wrote to his wife, Emma, at a difficult time. "In him I shall find comfort. I have given my life into his hands. I am prepared to go at his call. I desire to be with Christ. I count not my life dear to me, only to do his will." (In Dean C. Jessee, ed., *The Personal Writings of Joseph Smith*, p. 239, punctuation standardized.) Such expressions enable us to discern the soul of Joseph Smith, to discover the underlying secret of his success—his humility. He knew, and he wanted all others to know, that he walked in the shadow of the Almighty. But he was the Prophet of the Almighty; God knew it and he knew it.

Anciently when Aaron and Miriam allowed themselves to be possessed of a critical spirit toward their brother, Moses, Jehovah declared: "If there be a prophet among you, I the Lord will make myself known unto him in a vision, and will speak unto him in a dream. My servant Moses is not so, who is faithful in all mine house. With him will I speak mouth to mouth, even apparently, and not in dark speeches; and the similitude of the Lord shall he behold: wherefore then were ye not afraid to speak against my servant Moses?" (Numbers 12:6–8.) From this exchange we learn an important principle: there are prophets and then there are prophets. The Apostle Paul explained that "the spirits of the prophets are subject to the prophets" (1 Corinthians 14:32). There is an order, a hierarchy if you will, even among those called as chosen oracles and mouthpieces of the Almighty.

Jesus Christ is the presiding High Priest. The Prophet Joseph Smith explained that after Christ in the government of the kingdom of God comes Adam, and then Noah (see *Teachings of the Prophet Joseph Smith*, p. 157). "You start out with the Lord Jesus," Elder Bruce R. McConkie observed, "and then you have Adam and Noah. Thereafter come the dispensation heads. Then you step down, appreciably, and come to prophets and apostles, to the elders of Israel, and to wise and good and sagacious men who have the spirit of light and understanding." ("This Generation Shall Have My Word Through You," in *Hearken, O Ye People*, p. 4.) Joseph Smith, like Adam, Enoch, Noah, Abraham, Moses, Jesus, and others, stands as a dispensation head. The dispensation head becomes the means by which the knowledge and power of God are channeled to men and women on earth. He becomes the means by which the gospel of Jesus Christ—the plan of salvation and exaltation—is revealed anew, the means by which divine transforming powers, including saving covenants and ordinances, are extended to people during an age of time we call a dispensation. The dispensation head stands as the preeminent revealer and witness of Christ; he knows firsthand because of what he has seen and heard and felt and experienced. Because of his central place in the plan, because it is by means of the power of his testimony that men and women come to know the Lord and bask in the light of the Spirit, the calling and position of the dispensation head become something about which his followers feel to bear witness. Indeed, and appropriately so, men and women of a particular dispensation who stand to express the witness which burns in their bosoms find themselves bearing testimony of Christ and of the dispensation head—the revealer of Christ—in almost the same breath. This is just as it should be. Elder McConkie thus pointed out: "Every prophet is a witness of Christ; every dispensation head is a revealer of Christ for his day; and every other prophet or apostle who comes is a reflection and an echo and an exponent of the dispensation head. All such come to echo to the world and to expound and unfold what God has revealed through the man who was appointed for that era to give his eternal word to the world. Such is the dispensation concept." ("This Generation Shall Have My Word Through You," pp. 4–5.)

Thus to Joseph Smith the Savior declared, "This generation shall have my word through you" (D&C 5:10). Thomas B. Marsh was instructed to "declare glad tidings of great joy unto this generation." And what did that entail? Was Thomas to restate the Sermon on the Mount? Was he to reemphasize the poignant message in our Savior's Bread of Life Sermon? Was he to discuss at length the Lord's teachings at the Last Supper? No; his witness and his declaration were to be current. "You shall declare the things which have been revealed to my servant, Joseph Smith, Jun." (D&C 31:3–4.) If the knowledge and power of God are to be had in this final dispensation, they will be had through the work set in motion and the truths which flowed and the authorities which were transmitted by Joseph Smith, or they will be had not at all. To bear witness that Joseph Smith was a prophet is to testify that (1) he was a revealer of truth, divine truth, and more particularly the truths concerning Jesus Christ; and (2) that he was a legal administrator, a conduit by which the keys of the kingdom of God have been conferred upon men after the long night of apostate darkness.

Occasionally we hear people complain that they hear too few testimonies of Christ and too many of Joseph Smith. To be sure, we worship the Father in the name of the Son; Christ our Lord is the way to the Father (see John 14:6), and his is the only name under heaven whereby man can be saved (see Acts 4:12; Mosiah 3:17). And yet, we have seen that the dispensation head is the preeminent revealer of Christ. Thus to bear witness of Joseph Smith is to bear witness of Jesus Christ who sent him, in the same way that a testimony of Christ also implies clearly a testimony of the Eternal Father who sent him. On the other hand, to deny Joseph Smith outright—to deny the spiritual impressions which attest to his prophetic assignment—is to deny the Lord who sent him. Jesus told his disciples that "he that despiseth you despiseth me; and he that despiseth me despiseth him that sent me" (Luke 10:16; compare D&C 1:38; 84:36; 112:20). President Brigham Young thus testified that "whosoever confesseth that Joseph Smith was sent of God to reveal the holy Gospel to the children of men, and lay the foundation for gathering Israel, and building up the kingdom of God on the earth, that spirit is of God; and every spirit that does not confess that God has sent Joseph Smith, and revealed the everlasting Gospel to and through him, is of Antichrist, no matter whether it is found in a pulpit or on a throne" (*Journal of Discourses* 8:176). I have observed that there is a power—a supernal power, an unusual spiritual endowment from that Lord we worship—associated with the bearing of a pure and fervent testimony of Joseph Smith and the Restoration. Such outpourings surely signify heaven's approbation. President Joseph F. Smith, nephew of the Prophet, declared: "I believe in the divinity of Jesus Christ, because more than ever I come nearer the possession of the actual knowledge that Jesus is the Christ, the Son of the living God, through the testimony of Joseph Smith . . . that he saw Him, that he heard Him, that he received instructions from Him, that he obeyed those instructions, and that he today stands before the world as the last great, actual, living, witness of the divinity of Christ's mission and [Christ's] power to redeem man. . . . Thank God for Joseph Smith." (*Gospel Doctrine*, p. 495.)

Christ and His Anointed Servants

As Latter-day Saints, we have a living and current witness of Christ. We have the Bible, the Old Testament and the New Testament. They testify—particularly the New Testament testifies—that Jesus of Nazareth was and is the promised Messiah, the Son of God. We cherish what is there and gladly accept their witness. We thank God with all our heart for the knowledge of God and the testimony of Jesus that have been preserved by good and faithful men and women over the generations. But it is not enough. The revelation that came to Peter and James and John, the knowledge from heaven that settled upon the souls of Andrew and Simon and Nathaniel—as important as these things are, they are not sufficient to establish the doctrine of Christ in this last dispensation. We require a living tree of life. We know that Jesus is the Christ, not because the New Testament Apostles and prophets say so but because God has revealed his Son anew in our day and age through modern prophets, through living oracles.

Some five and one half centuries before the birth of Jesus, the American prophet Nephi, as a part of his farewell, set forth a vital principle. He wrote: "And now, my beloved brethren, and also Jew, and all ye ends of the earth, hearken unto these words and believe in Christ; and if ye believe not in these words believe in Christ. And if ye shall believe in Christ ye will believe in these words, for they are the words of Christ, and he hath given them unto me; and they teach all men that they should do good." (2 Nephi 33:10; compare Mormon 7:9.) To say this another way, those who truly love the Lord, who delight in his words and cherish his counsel; those whose hearts are open and receptive to truth and righteousness; those who feel no need to place bounds and limits upon the Almighty and say "Thus far and no more!"—these are they who shall recognize in the Book of Mormon the words and power of Jesus Christ.

In 1981 Elder Bruce R. McConkie asked the following personal and pertinent questions of the religious world:

> If you had lived in Jerusalem in the days of Jesus, would you have accepted him as the Son of God as did Peter and the Apostles? Or would you have said he had a devil and wrought miracles by the power of Beelzebub, as Annas and Caiaphas claimed?
>
> If you had lived in Nazareth or Cana or Capernaum, would you have believed the new religion preached by a few simple fishermen? Or would you have followed the traditions of your fathers in which there was no salvation?
>
> If you had lived in Corinth or Ephesus or Rome, would you have believed the strange new gospel preached by Paul? Or would you have put your trust in the vagaries and traditions and forms of worship that then prevailed?
>
> If you now live in New York or London or Paris, if you live in Chicago, Los Angeles, or Salt Lake—will you accept the new yet old religion, the new yet old gospel, the new yet old way of life that God has revealed anew for our day? Or will you sustain and support churches that no longer have any real resemblance to the one set up among the primitive Saints?
>
> If you hear a prophetic voice, if an apostolic witness is borne in your presence, if the servants of the Lord give you a message from their Master—what is your reaction? Do you believe or disbelieve?
>
> If you are told in words of soberness that Joseph Smith was called of God, that through him the fulness of the everlasting gospel has been restored, and that the Lord has established his church once again among men—do you believe the heaven-sent word? Or, like Annas and Caiaphas, do you stay with the status quo and trust your eternal salvation to the varying forms of man-made worship that abound on every hand?

After bearing witness of the Restoration, Elder McConkie continued:

Now, as Isaiah expressed it, "Who hath believed our report? and to whom is the arm of the Lord revealed?" (Isaiah 53:1.)

Who will believe our words, and who will hear our message? Who will honor the name of Joseph Smith and accept the gospel restored through his instrumentality?

We answer: the same people who would have believed the words of the Lord Jesus and the ancient Apostles and prophets had they lived in their day.

If you believe the words of Joseph Smith, you would have believed what Jesus and the ancients said.

If you reject Joseph Smith and his message, you would have rejected Peter and Paul and their message.

If you accept the prophets whom the Lord sends in your day, you also accept that Lord who sent them.

If you reject the restored gospel and find fault with the plan of salvation taught by those whom God hath sent in these last days, you would have rejected those same teachings as they fell from the lips of the prophets and Apostles of old. (Conference Report, October 1981, pp. 65–66, 68–69.)

There is no separating the Lord Jesus Christ from his anointed servants. The same spirit that testifies that Jesus Christ is the Son of the Living God and that he was crucified for the sins of the world testifies that Joseph Smith was called of God; that the Book of Mormon and the revelations and translations of the Restoration contain the mind and will and voice of the Lord; that angelic ministrants have visited the earth and restored knowledge and priesthood powers to legal administrators; that The Church of Jesus Christ of Latter-day Saints is the kingdom of God on earth and is, in the language of the revelation, "the only true and living church upon the face of the whole earth" (D&C 1:30); and that those called and empowered to be witnesses of the name of Christ in all the world—his modern Apostles and prophets—are in communication with that Lord they represent, and thus their words are to be received as though they were the very words of Christ himself.

To accept the servants of the Lord is to accept the Lord. To oppose or deny his servants is to oppose or deny him who sent them. There are some who have supposed, in their naiveté, that they can somehow come unto Christ and enjoy some special friendship with him while at the same time spurning and rejecting the words and the counsel of his living Apostles and prophets. There are even those members who speak of enjoying the blessings of the gospel in their personal lives, but who feel they have no need for The Church of Jesus Christ of Latter-day Saints. These are mistaken. They are deceived. They are walking in slippery paths along the road to personal apostasy.

The Church of Jesus Christ administers the gospel of Jesus Christ. The Church extends the ordinances and the covenants of salvation to the people of the earth. Though it is true that the power unto life and salvation is to be found in Christ the Person, such powers are only to be accessed through the divine program we know as the kingdom of God on earth. Further, loyalty to the Lord's anointed is prerequisite to loyalty to the Lord himself. It is worthy of note that the Risen Lord's extended list of Beatitudes among the Nephites begins with, "Blessed are ye if ye shall give heed unto the words of these twelve whom I have chosen from among you to minister unto you, and to be your servants" (3 Nephi 12:1). And in our day, in speaking of the required loyalty to the highest council of the Church, the Savior declared, "Whosoever receiveth my word receiveth me, and whosoever receiveth me, receiveth those, the First Presidency, whom I have sent" (D&C 112:20).

The Testimony of Modern Prophets

Can any person who is a genuine seeker after truth, who listens with his heart as well as his ears, observe the teachings and practices and doings of the Latter-day Saints and conclude that we are not Christian? Can any honest soul hear the words of witness of those called and endowed to bear a special witness and not know that Jesus Christ is at the heart of this work referred to as Mormonism? Consider the power and simple eloquence of testimony of but a few of those called as prophets, seers, and revelators:

> And now, after the many testimonies which have been given of him, this is the testimony, last of all, which we give of him: That he lives!
>
> For we saw him, even on the right hand of God; and we heard the voice bearing record that he is the Only Begotten of the Father—
>
> That by him, and through him, and of him, the worlds are and were created, and the inhabitants thereof are begotten sons and daughters unto God. (Joseph Smith, D&C 76:22–24.)

> I know that God lives. I know that Jesus lives; for I have seen Him. I know that this is the Church of God, and that it is founded on Jesus Christ, our Redeemer. I testify to you of these things as one that knows—as one of the Apostles of the Lord Jesus Christ that can bear witness to you today in the presence of the Lord that He lives and that He will live, and will come to reign on the earth, to sway an undisputed sceptre. (George Q. Cannon, *Gospel Truth*, p. 106.)

> There has come to me in these last few days a deepening and reassuring faith. I can't leave this conference without saying to you that I have a conviction that the Master hasn't been absent from us on these occasions. This is his church. Where else would he rather be than right here at the headquarters of his church? He isn't an absentee master; he is concerned about us. He wants us to follow where he leads. I know that he is a living reality, as is our Heavenly Father. I know it. (Harold B. Lee, Conference Report, October 1972, p. 176.)

And now, as pertaining to this perfect atonement, wrought by the shedding of the blood of God—I testify that it took place in Gethsemane and at Golgotha, and as pertaining to Jesus Christ, I testify that he is the Son of the Living God and was crucified for the sins of the world. He is our Lord, our God, and our King. This I know of myself independent of any other person.

I am one of his witnesses, and in a coming day I shall feel the nail marks in his hands and in his feet and shall wet his feet with my tears.

But I shall not know any better then than I know now that he is God's Almighty Son, that he is our Savior and Redeemer, and that salvation comes in and through his atoning blood and in no other way. (Bruce R. McConkie, Conference Report, April 1985, p. 12.)

Gladly and unashamedly, I add my small voice to the anthem of apostolic appreciation by acknowledging and adoring Jesus of Nazareth, Savior and King.

I witness that *He lives*—with all that those simple words imply—knowing that I will be held accountable for this testimony; but, as readers, you are now accountable for my witness, which I give in love and sobriety. (Neal A. Maxwell, *Even As I Am,* pp. 121–22.)

Now, I wonder with you why one such as I should be called to the holy apostleship. There are so many qualifications that I lack. There is so much in my effort to serve that is wanting. As I have pondered on it, I have come to only one single thing, one qualification in which there may be cause, and that is, I have *that* witness.

I declare to you that I know that Jesus is the Christ. I know that He lives. He was born in the meridian of time. He taught His gospel, was tried, was crucified. He rose on the third day. He was the first fruits of the Resurrection. He has a body of flesh and bone. Of this I bear testimony. Of Him I am a witness. (Boyd K. Packer, Conference Report, April 1971, p. 125.)

I testify that He is a teacher of truth—but He is more than a teacher. He is the exemplar of the perfect life—but He is more than an exemplar. He is the great physician—but He is more than a physician. He is the literal Savior of the world, the Son of God, the Prince of Peace, the Holy One of Israel, even the risen Lord. . . . As His witness, I testify to you that he lives! (Thomas S. Monson, "Invitation to Exaltation," p. 6.)

I believe that in [Christ's] mortal life he was the one perfect man to walk the earth. I believe that in his words are to be found that light and truth which, if observed, would save the world and bring exaltation to mankind. . . .

None so great has ever walked the earth. None other has made a comparable sacrifice or granted a comparable blessing. He is the Savior and the Redeemer of the world. I believe in him. I declare his divinity without equivocation or compromise. I love him. I speak his name in reverence and wonder. I worship him as I worship his Father, in spirit and in truth. I thank him and kneel before his wounded feet and hands and side, amazed at the love he offers me. . . .

This is the Christ in whom I believe and of whom I testify.

That knowledge comes from the word of scripture, and that testimony comes by the power of the Holy Ghost. (Gordon B. Hinckley, *Faith, the Essence of True Religion,* pp. 24, 25.)

We testify as the ancient prophets and Apostles did, that the name of Christ is the only name given under heaven whereby a man, woman, or child can be saved. It is a blessed name, a gracious name, a sacred name. . . .

. . . Sooner or later, and we pray sooner *than* later, everyone will acknowledge that Christ's way is not only the *right* way, but ultimately the *only* way to hope and joy. Every knee shall bow and every tongue will confess that gentleness is better than brutality, that kindness is greater than coercion, that the soft voice turneth away wrath. In the end, and sooner than that whenever possible, we must be more like him.

. . . I testify that Jesus is the only true source of lasting joy, that our only lasting peace is in him. (Howard W. Hunter, Conference Report, April 1993, pp. 79–80.)

The question is sometimes asked, "Are Mormons Christians?" We declare the divinity of Jesus Christ. We look to Him as the only source of our salvation. We strive to live His teachings, and we look forward to the time that He shall come again on this earth to rule and reign as King of Kings and Lord of Lords. . . .

We should like to reaffirm to all the world that The Church of Jesus Christ of Latter-day Saints is led by our Lord and Savior, Jesus Christ. We believe in Christ. We accept and affirm His teachings as revealed truths from God. We know Him to be the literal Son of God. We love Him as our resurrected Lord and Savior. (Ezra Taft Benson, *The Teachings of Ezra Taft Benson*, pp. 10, 12.)

The Center of Our Faith

This system of salvation that we know as Mormonism, this Church of Jesus Christ of Latter-day Saints, stands as a grand witness of him who came to ransom us from sin and death. This is Christ's church. It teaches his doctrines and administers his gospel. The Master is at the center, and all the other things—truths, doctrines, principles, and programs—find their meaning, purpose, substance, and power in and through him. For surely where there is no center, there can be no circumference. Indeed, Jesus Christ is the central figure in the doctrine and practice of the Latter-day Saints. We claim no historical attachment to or doctrinal dependence upon the Christian churches of the world. We share only our assurance that Jesus of Nazareth was and is the Savior of all mankind. He lives, and we know it.

CHAPTER 1

On Being Christian

I was born and reared in the southern states and attended Louisiana State University for two years. Those two years were perhaps the loneliest time of my life. In spite of what many have said, for me the 1960s was a terrible time to grow up in. By the time I had graduated from high school the Beatles and British music had taken the world by storm. The other type of music that survived the revolution was folk music, where everyone sang or chanted about the economy, the Vietnam War, and nuclear holocaust. Really depressing stuff! Many of the movies dealt with social issues, and few had happy endings. It was a time of revolution, and everyone seemed to be in search of a cause, a crusade of some type. Marches and sit-ins and protests abounded.

In addition, I was a part of the "baby boom" generation that arrived at the college campus before we were ready to be received. Institutions of higher learning literally did not have the resources to meet the flood of young people that hit the campus. Consequently, many universities set up a type of selection process, a means whereby only the most serious and dedicated students would make it through the first year. For example, of the 4,300 freshmen who entered with me in the fall of 1965 at LSU, about 1,800 continued as sophomores. Freshman Biology and Freshman English were the designated "flunkout" courses. To be honest, although I was very happy in high school, I did not enjoy my first years of college. I felt very much alone.

After my mission I transferred to Brigham Young University and fell in love with the Provo community and with BYU. For someone who as a boy had gotten no closer to the Salt Lake Temple than an Articles of Faith card, there was something special about being so near the headquarters of the Church. Every Tuesday there was a devotional on the campus, and almost always one of the General Authorities of the Church was the speaker. I loved each of those devotionals; in my files I still have copies of the addresses. I thrilled at the idea of having prayer in some of my classes. I can't explain it, but there was something strange and unusual, something marvelous about being on a large university campus among thousands of people who believed basically the same things about life that I did.

My earliest class was an 8:00 a.m. Monday-Wednesday-Friday class, "An Introduction to Philosophy." The instructor was excellent; he was warm and accommodating and patient with us as students. About three weeks into the semester, I approached him on a matter we had covered during the hour. "What can I do for you?" he asked. I posed my question. He looked at his watch. Memories of disinterested and discourteous teachers from other places flooded back into my mind, and my heart began to beat a little faster. I fully expected him to say: "I'm a busy man. Don't bother me at times other than my office hours!" Instead, he asked: "What are you doing this hour? Do you have a class?" I answered that I was free for two hours. "Come on," he said, as he began to leave the classroom, "walk with me to the Wilkinson Center [the Student Union]—I'll buy you something to drink, and we'll talk about it." It was a tender and important moment for me, one that comes back frequently when I'm busy, tired, and being summoned by a troubled student. It was a simple act of courtesy and concern; it was a quiet, Christian deed, and it made all the difference in the world to me. I felt at home, at peace on campus, and my grades showed it.

The spirit of that little incident drives what I feel today. I speak of being Christian, followers of him who has taught us to reach out, lift up, and embrace those who need us. The incident epitomizes for me what can exist among people, how men and women, how Latter-day Saints and those not of that faith, can live together in love and harmony.

On Being a True Christian

Maybe it would be helpful, to begin with, to suggest what being Christian is *not*. It is easy to become caught up in many of the trappings of Christendom, to become enamored with so much of what so many feel to be Christian activity. For example, a Christian is not necessarily one who is so nice, so sweet, so milquetoast that people trample over him or her. Jesus was not a doormat, and he certainly did not call his disciples to be doormats. He has asked us to be patient, to avoid confrontations and disputations where such is possible, but he never asked us to roll over and play dead while others take advantage of us.

Nor is a Christian necessarily one who is so broad-minded, so eager to celebrate diversity, so tolerant, so pluralistic, that he or she cannot hold to principle or embrace the full truth. Elder Dallin H. Oaks has explained:

Other strengths that can be used for our downfall are the gifts of love and tolerance. Clearly, these are great virtues. Love is an ultimate quality, and tolerance is its handmaiden. Love and tolerance are pluralistic, and that is their strength, but it is also the source of their potential weakness. Love and tolerance are incomplete unless they are accompanied by a concern for truth and a commitment to the unity God has commanded of his servants.

Carried to an undisciplined excess, love and tolerance can produce indifference to truth and justice and opposition to unity. What makes mankind "free" from death and sin is not merely love but love accompanied by truth: "And ye shall know the truth, and the truth shall make you free" (John 8:32). And *the test of whether we are the Lord's is not just love and tolerance, but unity.* "If ye are not one," the risen Lord said, "ye are not mine" (D&C 38:27). ("Our Strengths Can Become Our Downfall," p. 114, emphasis added.)

A Christian is not necessarily one who champions every cause and leads every crusade. In fact, one of the great needs of this age is for persons possessed of the Spirit of God to be discerning, not alone in knowing good from evil but also in sensing what things matter more than others. In a word, with so very many pressing needs, so very many enterprises that beckon for a leader or for followers, it is essential that we spend our days laboring in primary causes. It would be tragic indeed to finish our lives and then realize that the majority of our waking moments had been spent in secondary causes. In this connection, only four months after the Watergate scandal had become public Elder Bruce R. McConkie said in general conference:

In view of all that prevails in the world, it might be easy to center our attention on negative or evil things, or to dissipate our energies on causes and enterprises of doubtful worth and questionable productivity.

I am fully aware of the divine decree to be actively engaged in a good cause; of the fact that every true principle which works for the freedom and blessing of mankind has the Lord's approval; of the need to sustain and support those who espouse proper causes and advocate true principles—all of which things we also should do in the best and most beneficial way we can. The issue, I think, is not *what* we should do but *how* we should do it; and I maintain that the most beneficial and productive thing which Latter-day Saints can do to strengthen every good and proper cause is to live and teach the principles of the everlasting gospel. (Conference Report, October 1973, p. 55.)

The problem with the "social gospel movement," the effort to take Christendom into society and make of Christian theology a relevant religion, is that such an enterprise is, and will be forevermore, deficient. Permanent change is in Christ the Person, not in programs. Christ can impact society only to the degree that he is allowed to impact individual souls. As President Ezra Taft Benson observed: "The Lord works from the inside out. The world works from the outside in. The world would take people out of the slums. Christ takes the slums out of people, and then they take themselves out of the slums. The world would mold men by changing their environment. Christ changes men, who then change their environment. The world would shape human behavior, but Christ can change human nature." (Conference Report, April 1985, p. 5.)

One Protestant writer, John Stott, has beautifully described the importance of extending the full blessings of Christianity to those who are in need: "If a vagrant comes to us in dire need, down and out, in rags and tatters, and sick, even starving, it will be good to give him a bath and a change of clothing, but not enough. For he is ill and undernourished. So, in addition, he needs food and hospital treatment. Similarly, we come to Christ down and out, in the rags and tatters of our sin, spiritually sick and starving. In Christ we are at once made welcome and accepted, and given a bath and a change of clothes. God sees us as righteous in Christ. This is our new status. But it is only the beginning. The Good Physician knows we are sick. So he puts his Spirit within us to give us new life and health, and he feeds us with his word until we grow strong and vigorous. There are no half-measures with him." (*Life in Christ*, p. 44.)

In the truest sense, one is a Christian when he or she fully believes that Jesus of Nazareth was and is the Son of God, the Savior and Redeemer, the Christ or Anointed One. A Christian is one who knows by the witness of the Holy Spirit that Christ is God, that he laid down his life by the power of the flesh and took it up again by the power of the Spirit. A Christian is one who calls upon the Father in the name of the Son for forgiveness, forsakes sin and indecency, and yearns to qualify for that new life that comes through redemption and renovation of the soul. A Christian is one whose commitment to Christ is such that he or she strives daily to become as Christ is, to acquire that nature and to embody those spiritual attributes and qualities that flow from him in whom all fulness and perfection dwell. A Christian, in other words, is not just one who does good deeds, as important as that is. It is one who accepts the doctrine of Christ, takes the name of Christ, and seeks thereafter to do the works of Christ. Goodness and decency and compassion are the natural by-products, the fruits that readily manifest themselves in the lives of those who have truly made Jesus their Lord and Master.

On Giving and Taking Offense

In the mid-nineteen-seventies my family and I moved to the South to assume the direction of the institute of religion adjacent to the university there. I was asked to replace a man who had become an institution—among both his students and the members of the stake in which he served. He had become one of the most beloved of teachers I have ever known. A few days after our arrival, it be-

"Jesus in the Synagogue at Nazareth," by Greg K. Olsen.
Courtesy of Leo and Annette Beus.

"Christ Calls Two Disciples," by Gary E. Smith.

came very clear that taking his place would not be easy. A student stopped by my office and, with a frightened look in his eye, asked: "Where's Brother Jensen?" I answered that he had moved from the area. "Moved from the area? Well, who's going to take his place?" I meekly admitted that I would try to do so. "Oh, terrific!" he came right back. The overall reception was not exactly cold, but rather a bit guarded. For three weeks students came into the place asking about Brother Jensen, some mourning about his departure, others observing sadly that they had enjoyed institute very much up until now.

My wife, Shauna, and I were asked to speak in sacrament meeting in our new ward. We did so, and I thought it went fairly well. After the benediction's "Amen" was said, I noticed a man from the congregation walking very quickly to the stand. He reached out his right hand, shook mine, and said: "Hello. My name is Alex Campbell. My family was very, very close to the Jensens. I would like to say that you will never replace Brother Jensen as a speaker or a teacher, but we will try to love you anyway."

I waited for him to smile, supposing that he was teasing. He did not smile, but simply left the stand and returned to his family. The member of the bishopric conducting the meeting hastened to my side and explained that, indeed, the two families had become very close.

I remember going to the bedroom when my wife and I got home, lying on the bed, and crying. I said to her: "Why won't they at least give me a chance?" For a day or two, I am ashamed to admit, I had unkind feelings toward Alex Campbell. He was the straw that had broken the camel's back. It is important that you understand that my family and I came to love that part of the country more than any place we had lived, and, ironically, Alex became one of my dearest and closest friends.

To show you that Alex didn't change a great deal even after we became quite close, I relate the following. About six months after we had moved from the area, Alex and his family came to visit us in our new home during the Christmas season. I opened the door to welcome them and Brother Campbell looked into our home. His opening words were: "I've never cared for artificial Christmas trees!" I came to love him like a brother (and still do), not because all of his comments to me or mine were complimentary, nor because his style or taste or manner was just like mine. No, once I knew his heart, once I knew who he was and how much he cared, I felt no reason to take offense. I knew he had no desire to give offense, and so I chose to love him in spite of himself.

A few years after I had joined the faculty at BYU I had an experience that caused me much pain at the time. A man came to my office and indicated that he had heard that Joseph McConkie and I had published a book on life after death. I nodded. He then said: "I wonder if I might borrow a copy for a few days to see if it's something I might want to buy." I was a bit startled by the request but sheepishly complied and provided a copy of the book for him. Three days later he dropped by, slid the book across the desk, and said: "I've looked it over and decided that I don't want to buy it!" To say that I was hurt would be the grossest of understatements. I wasn't too angry, nor did I pout for too long. Most of all I was shocked. Shaken. And, of course, hurt. But I add quickly that this person and I now have a wonderful relationship.

I have feelings, just as the next person has. I have been insulted, belittled, put down in front of others. I know what it feels like to be misunderstood, to have my motives or my intentions questioned. In other words, I know what it feels like to be offended.

As to giving and taking offense, on the one hand, you and I need to be more sensitive, more cautious with people's feelings. We need to do all in our power to keep from excluding others, to keep from making people feel left out. We need to show respect and dignity to individuals, regardless of their color, their personal beliefs, their religion, or their gender. We are all human beings, sons and daughters of God first and foremost; these things we share with every other mortal. God loves us all, and, as the scriptures affirm, he is no respecter of persons. Christians do not shun others whose religious or political views are different from their own, any more than the Lord Jesus Christ would shun people. The Prophet Joseph Smith taught: "There is a love from God that should be exercised toward those of our faith, who walk uprightly, which is peculiar to itself, but it is without prejudice; it also gives scope to the mind, which enables us to conduct ourselves with greater liberality towards all that are not of our faith, than what they exercise towards one another. These principles approximate nearer to the mind of God, because [they are] like God, or Godlike." (*Teachings of the Prophet Joseph Smith*, p. 147.)

There is, of course, another side to this story. In order to live in harmony, we must become the kind of people who are not constantly looking to take offense. Each of us could easily waste our lives striving to make our associates offenders for a word. Many times each day we could take offense at the way we are spoken to (or not spoken to), the way we are introduced, the way someone mispronounces our name, or the way we feel we are ignored or overlooked. In the United States our society's inability to be fully Christian has led to a staggering increase in the number of court cases. Everyone wants to sue someone, it seems. We have become a litigious people, a nation that thinks first of justice and later (if at all) of reconciliation or even forgiveness (see Dallin H. Oaks, *The Lord's Way*, pp. 157–58). Our tendency to look for and take offense has made it extremely difficult to function in society, even to the point at which individuals are frightened to speak, anxious about saying anything, for fear that their language or their approach is not "politically correct." One of the ironic realities of our day—and this is particularly true in modern universities—is that an overmuch dose of multiculturalism and an exaggerated stress on diversity can create a type of ethnicity that will in time contribute to the segregation and disunity of our society. Such separatism "nourishes prejudices, magnifies differences and stirs antagonisms." (Arthur M. Schlesinger, Jr., *The Disuniting of America*, p. 17.) Christians need not fall prey to such trends.

I have come to know that we need not be offended, that one of the most important signs of spiritual growth is a refusal to take offense. We need not be angry or bitter or insulted. We need not make our sister or our brother an offender for a word. It really is not too difficult to look at a person's heart, to try to understand what he meant to do rather than what he did, or what she meant to say rather than what she said. Sometimes this entails simply looking the other way and assuming the best. Sometimes it requires forgiveness. President Gordon B. Hinckley pointed out that there is no virtue more needed in our day than forgiving and forgetting. "There are those who would look upon this as a sign of weakness. Is it? I submit that it takes neither strength nor intelligence to brood in anger over wrongs suffered, to go through life with a spirit of vindictiveness, to dissipate one's abilities in planning retribution. There is no peace in the nursing of a grudge." (*Ensign*, June 1991, p. 4.) To strive earnestly not to offend is a Christian virtue. To strive earnestly not to take offense is a Christian virtue at least as important. We need both virtues desperately.

On Being a Friend to All

Jesus ate and drank with sinners. He occasionally companied with those who were considered to be in the lower crust of society. He befriended the underdog and was kind to the castoff. Because there was no insecurity within him, because he was guided always by the knowledge of who he was and whose he was, he felt no need to put on airs, manage appearances, or be socially selective. When someone spoke to Jesus, surely they had his full attention.

It is so easy for those of us who aspire to Christian discipleship to be driven by what others think, to allow our conversation and our conduct to be determined by less than noble motives. It is so simple to be drawn into duplicity, to become obsessed with whose opinion matters and whose company would bring the most mortal medals. But the lowly Nazarene calls us to a higher righteousness. He bids us to follow where he has led, to become a friend to all. I know what it feels like to be conversing with someone, only to have that conversation interrupted by a man or woman of greater social stature. I know what it feels like for the person with whom I was conversing to then ignore or shun me, to turn his attention to the one who seems to matter most at the moment. I also have been in the presence of persons whose hearts are unconcerned with society's pecking order, men and women who love people, not position. In the former category of persons are those who tend to distinguish people in terms of rank and place in society; theirs is a degrading and demoralizing perspective and influence. On the other hand, those who have risen above the temptation to exclude or divide or distinguish in terms of getting ahead make a significant difference in the world.

On Being Inconvenienced

The call to follow Christ is a call to inconvenience. Some things simply take time. They take effort. Doing for others generally entails putting on hold what one had planned to do for oneself. In the seventh chapter of Mark we read the following: "And from thence [Jesus] arose, and went into the borders of Tyre and Sidon, and entered into an house, and would have no man know it: but he could not be hid." The account continues by explaining that a certain woman found Jesus and pleaded with him to heal her daughter (Mark 7:24–26).

It appears that our Lord was tired, weary, in need of rest and peace and solitude. The Joseph Smith Translation of this passage is most instructive: "And from thence he arose, and went into the borders of Tyre and Sidon, and entered into a house, and would that no man should come unto him. But he could not deny them; for he had compassion upon all men." (JST, Mark 7:22–23.) It is inconceivable that the Redeemer of the world couldn't have hidden himself if he had wanted to. He is the God of the universe and has power over the elements. It is unthinkable that he could not have concealed himself in some way, *except* that his compassion for his brothers and sisters would not allow him to do so. Our Savior was willing to be inconvenienced. And so must we be, if we are to become as he is. Such inconvenience may take many forms, some quite simple, others more dramatic. We may offer to assist a fellow member of the Church who is struggling with a particular principle; sincerely befriend someone not of our faith, even if he or she has no intention whatsoever of joining the LDS church; or take the time to visit and cheer up someone who is homesick, lonely, or depressed.

Sometimes all we can do is wish we could help (see Mosiah 4:24). At least that's a start. Elder Boyd K. Packer told of an experience he had while in the military. After being stationed for a time in Japan, the day came when he had to leave. Of this experience he said:

> I boarded a train in Osaka for Yokohama and a ship that would take me home. . . .
>
> It was a very chilly night. The railroad station, what there was left of it, was very cold. Starving children were sleeping in the corners. That was a common sight in Japan in those days. The fortunate ones had a newspaper or a few old rags to fend off the cold.
>
> On that train I slept restlessly. The berths were too short

anyway. In the bleak, chilly hours of the dawn, the train stopped at a station along the way. I heard a tapping on the window and raised the blind. There on the platform stood a little boy tapping on the window with a tin can. I knew he was one of the orphans and a beggar; the tin can was the symbol of their suffering. Sometimes they carried a spoon as well, as if to say, "I am hungry; feed me."

He might have been six or seven years old. His little body was thin with starvation. He had on a thin, ragged shirt-like kimono, nothing else. His head was shingled with scabs. One side of his jaw was swollen—perhaps from an abscessed tooth. Around his head he had tied a filthy rag with a knot on top of his head—a pathetic gesture of treatment.

When I saw him and he saw that I was awake, he waved his can. He was begging. In pity, I thought, "How can I help him?" Then I remembered. I had money, Japanese money. I quickly groped for my clothing and found some yen notes in my pocket. I tried to open the window, but it was stuck. I slipped on my trousers and hurried to the end of the car. He stood outside expectantly. As I pushed at the resistant door, the train pulled away from the station. Through the dirty windows I could see him, holding that rusty tin can, with the dirty rag around his swollen jaw.

There I stood, an officer from a conquering army, heading home to a family and a future. There I stood, half-dressed, clutching some money which he had seen, but which I could not get to him. I wanted to help him, but couldn't. The only comfort I draw is that I did want to help him.

"Perhaps I was scarred by that experience," Elder Packer concluded. "If so, it is a battle scar, a worthy one, for which I bear no shame. It reminds me of my duty." (*Let Not Your Heart Be Troubled*, pp. 35–36.)

In January 1982 at Washington's National Airport, Air Florida's Flight 90 to Tampa crashed into the Fourteenth Street Bridge and slid into the Potomac River with seventy-four passengers aboard. In *Time* magazine, a reporter explained:

For a moment, there was silence, and then pandemonium. Commuters watched helplessly as the plane quickly sank. . . . A few passengers bobbed to the surface; some clung numbly to pieces of debris while others screamed desperately for help. Scattered across the ice were pieces of green upholstery, twisted chunks of metal, luggage, a tennis racket, a child's shoe. . . .

Within minutes, sirens began to wail as fire trucks, ambulances and police cars rushed to the scene. A U.S. Park Police helicopter hovered overhead to pluck survivors out of the water. Six were clinging to the plane's tail. Dangling a life preserving ring to them, the chopper began ferrying them to shore. One woman had injured her right arm, so [the] pilot . . . lowered the copter until its skids touched the water; his partner [then leaped out and] scooped her up in his arms. Then [a young woman] grabbed the preserver, but as she was being helped out of the . . . river by [a] fellow passenger . . . she lost her grip. . . . A clerk for the Congressional Budget Office who was watching from the shore plunged into the water and dragged her to land. But the most notable act of heroism was performed by [another] of the passengers, a balding man in his early 50s. Each time the ring was lowered, he grabbed it and passed it along to a comrade; when the helicopter finally returned to pick him up, he had disappeared beneath the ice. (James Kelly, "We're Not Going to Make It," pp. 16–17.)

In that same issue of *Time*, another writer described the unknown man in the water:

His selflessness [is] one reason the story held national attention; his anonymity another. The fact that he [has gone] unidentified invests him with a universal character. For a while he was Everyman, and thus proof (as if one needed it) that no man is ordinary.

Still, he could never have imagined such a capacity in himself. Only minutes before his character was tested, he was sitting in the ordinary plane among the ordinary passengers, dutifully listening to the stewardess telling him to fasten his seat belt and saying something about the "no smoking sign." So our man relaxed with the others, some of whom would owe their lives to him. Perhaps he started to read, or to doze, or to regret some harsh remark made in the office that morning. Then suddenly he knew that the trip would not be ordinary. Like every other person on that flight, he was desperate to live, which makes his final act so stunning.

For at some moment in the water he must have realized that he would not live if he continued to hand over the rope and ring to others. He *had* to know it, no matter how gradual the effect of the cold. In his judgment he had no choice. When the helicopter took off with what was to be the last survivor, he watched everything in [his] world move away from him, and he deliberately let it [go]. . . .

The odd thing is that we do not . . . really believe that the man in the water lost his fight. . . . He could not [like Nature], make ice storms, or freeze the water until it froze the blood. But he could hand life over to a stranger, and that is a power of nature too. The man in the water pitted himself against an implacable, impersonal enemy; he fought it with charity; and he [won]. (Roger Rosenblatt, "The Man in the Water," p. 86.)

Conclusion

The Savior expects us to do our part to assure that all we do in the Church is imbued with the religion of Jesus Christ. Almost a quarter of a century ago, President Hugh B. Brown observed: "Religion has too often spent a large proportion of its effort on doings apart from the real business of life. One of life's problems is to establish a deep understanding of man's relationship to his fellow men. . . . Every man's religion should have practical issue," he continued, "not merely emotional responsiveness which delights in hearing the gospel but lacks diligence in living it. We must remember that religion is action, not diction. Let us pray that God will deliver us from our dullness of conscience, from a feeble sense of duty, from thoughtless disregard of others, and from all halfheartedness in our work." (*Vision and Valor*, pp. 48, 50.)

People really matter. They matter more than anything. God is in the people business (see Moses 1:39), and we should be too. The story is told that Julia Ward Howe expressed a concern to a senator on one occasion, asking him to interest himself in the case of someone needing help. "Julia, I have become so busy," the man answered, "I can no longer concern myself with individuals." Her reply is so very pertinent to our day. "That's remarkable," she came back. "Even God hasn't reached that stage yet." (Cited in *Richard Evans' Quote Book*, p. 165.)

Is there someone out there who needs me? Do I know of someone who could use a friend, who would come alive on receiving an unassigned or unexpected phone call or visit? Do I treat those not of my faith with dignity, respect, and consideration, attempting earnestly never to exclude them or make them feel uncomfortable? "It is a serious thing," C. S. Lewis wrote, "to live in a society of possible gods and goddesses, to remember that the dullest and most uninteresting person you can talk to may one day be a creature which, if you saw it now, you would be strongly tempted to worship. . . . There are no *ordinary* people. You have never talked to a mere mortal. Nations, cultures, arts, civilization—these are mortal, and their life is to ours as the life of a gnat. But it is immortals whom we joke with, work with, marry, snub, and exploit." (*The Weight of Glory*, pp. 18–19.)

At the convocation for the College of Education at Brigham Young University in the summer of 1992, one of the students shared with her fellow graduates, and the others present, a touching story about an experience she had with a young native American boy. He had been stereotyped by previous teachers as incorrigible, as a serious problem. She felt impelled to reach out and help. She knew the family situation was difficult and thought that if she visited his home she might find some clue as to how to reach him. The experience stunned and sobered her. She found poverty, neglect, alcoholism, drug abuse—everything that is negative and destructive seemed to be present. Her heart ached for the boy; his situation made her despondent. As she poured her heart out in prayer to the Lord, she found herself asking, "Have you forgotten this boy?" Then the answer came, quietly and reassuringly: "No, that is why I sent you."

So very often the Almighty answers people's prayers— the prayers of the lonely, the downtrodden, the hungry, the bitter—through other people, through those sensitive souls who open themselves to inspiration and are willing to be inconvenienced. There are joys, supernal joys, that unfold in our lives as we learn to love others as we would desire to be loved. As we come to do so, we come unto him who is the embodiment of love.

CHAPTER 2

A Name Above All Other Names

In a world where upright, moral, God-fearing people would never even think of committing murder or theft or adultery, it is surprising how often the name of God is taken in vain without a second thought. Even among those in our society who are civic-minded and service-oriented, we too often hear the sacred name of God dragged through the gutter through being placed in an alien context—through flippant, profane, or unclean speech. Why is it that good people can be so observant of those Sinaitic commandments that pertain to interpersonal relationships but miss the mark of propriety when it comes to the dignity and sanctity that should attend the name and person of Deity? Taking the name of God in vain entails far more than profaning his name, more than cursing and blaspheming. It of course has something to do with the way we speak, but, more important, it has to do with the way we live and the way we are. It has to do with our eternal perspective, with the manner in which we think and act about sacred things. It has everything to do with the way we assume our covenantal responsibilities as Christians.

Taking His Name Upon Us

There is a name that is above every other name that is named, whether on earth or in heaven, save only the name of the Almighty Elohim (see Philippians 2:9–11). There is a name that brings joy to the desolate heart, a name that speaks peace to the sorrowing soul. There is a name that falls in hushed and hallowed tones from the lips of saints and angels, a name that leads true believers on both sides of the veil to glory and honor everlasting. It is the name of the One sent of God to bring salvation, the name of the One who paid the infinite price to ransom us from Satan's grasp. It is the blessed name of Jesus Christ.

The fall of Adam and Eve, though a fortunate fall and an essential step toward mortality and thus a pillar in the plan of salvation, brought about dramatic changes in the earth and all forms of life on it. The Fall introduced physical death—made inevitable the separation of man's spirit and body. It introduced spiritual death—made inevitable the separation of man from God and His environment of righteousness. As a result of the Fall, all mankind leave the premortal world to come forth into a fallen state, a telestial condition. Spiritual death represents an alienation from God, in a sense a disinheritance from the royal family. Unless appropriate reconciliation with the family head is made, the right to bear the family name may be lost. That is, unless an atonement is brought to pass, God's children lose that association and sociality, that family life of which the scriptures speak—eternal life. They are then nameless and familyless. They are spiritual orphans and thereby alone in the world; from an eternal perspective, in the words of Malachi, they are without root or branch (see

Malachi 4:1). In order to experience those joys and feel that warmth known only in family living, one must be reinstated in the family, redeemed, deemed worthy once again of the privileges and opportunities that result from being called a son or daughter of God.

Deliverance from the fallen state—redemption from spiritual death—is made available only through the labors and sufferings of a God, through the ministry of one mightier than death, one upon whom justice has no claims and death has no hold. Deliverance comes only through Jesus Christ. As the foreordained Messiah, Jesus our Savior became the "author of eternal salvation unto all them that obey him" (Hebrews 5:9), and the Father's gospel—the gospel of God (see Romans 1:1–3)—became his, the gospel of Jesus Christ. Christ is thus the Father of salvation, the Father of resurrection, the Father of redemption. He is also the King of kings, and admission into his family (through faith, repentance, baptism, the reception of the Holy Ghost, and a "mighty change" of heart—see Mosiah 5:2) represents acceptance into his family kingdom. Those who have thus been born again become members of the family of Christ and therefore take upon them the family name (see Mosiah 5:7)—they become Christians and are obligated by covenant to live in harmony with the requirements and standards of the family, to live a life befitting the new and holy name they have taken upon themselves. "Family members bear the family name," Elder Bruce R. McConkie wrote. "By it they are known and called and identified; it sets them apart from all those of a different lineage and ancestry. Adopted children take upon them the name of their newfound parents and become in all respects as though they had been born in the family. And so it is that the children of Christ, those who are born again, those who are spiritually begotten by their new Father, take upon themselves the name of Christ. . . . They are now family members, Christians in the real and true sense of the word." (*The Promised Messiah*, p. 363.)

Acting in His Name

An angel explained to father Adam nearly six millennia ago: "Thou shalt do all that thou doest in the name of the Son, and thou shalt repent and call upon God in the name of the Son forevermore" (Moses 5:8). We are to do all things in the name of the Son. *All* things. We are to speak and act and worship and perform the labors of the kingdom—all in the name of the Son. We are the servants of the Lord, who is our Master, and he has commanded us to labor in his fields—plowing, sowing, cultivating, and harvesting. That is, we are the *agents* of the Lord, who is our eternal *Principal*, and he has empowered us to represent him to do the things he would do if he were personally present. To do all things in his name in righteousness means that we put ourselves in his place and stead, that we strive to think and speak and act as though we were the One whose blessed name we bear. Our acts become his acts—they are done in his name.

It is an awesome responsibility to speak in the name of the Lord. The messengers of salvation are under obligation to "declare the word with truth and soberness" (Alma 42:31). That is, they are to be faithful to the spirit and intent of the message to be delivered. Nephi explained that those who are born again and speak under the influence of the Holy Ghost speak "with the tongue of angels"; they declare what angels would declare if they were present. Such persons thereby speak "the words of Christ" (2 Nephi 31:13; 32:1–3). While the Apostles and prophets stand as the examples and models of what all the Saints of the Most High should be and do in this regard, the everlasting gospel has been restored in our day "that every man might speak in the name of God the Lord, even the Savior of the world" (D&C 1:20).

God the Eternal Father has placed his name upon the Son (see John 5:43; 10:25). Thus, in using his Father's name Jesus made his words and acts those of his Father. There are numerous places of scripture in which Jesus, who is the Lord Jehovah, speaks in behalf of his Father in the first person as though he were the Almighty Elohim, using the very words of his Father. His doing so is an illustration of speaking by divine investiture of authority. Men and women who have been ordained or set apart to deliver the message of salvation—who have been commissioned to represent the Lord and proclaim the truths of his everlasting gospel—likewise may speak by divine investiture of authority. They do not necessarily declare, "Thus saith the Lord," and it is not necessary that they speak in the first person for the Father or for Jesus Christ, his Son. But they do stand as representatives and agents of their Master and as such are entitled to the quiet yet persuasive whisperings of the Holy Spirit, which, when they receive them, authorize and justify their utterances. God honors his servants. He vindicates the words of his chosen vessels (see Moses 6:32–34).

That Jesus performed ordinances is well known. He baptized, conferred the Holy Ghost, administered the sacrament, ordained men to priestly offices—all in the power and authority of his divine sonship. But he is not available to do these things for each individual, so he empowers others to act in his name—he extends an investiture of authority, if you will—to ensure that all have the privilege of receiving those powers and rites that enable us to become even as he is. To be valid, all ordinances must be performed by him or by his word—meaning, by his servants who act in his holy name. Thus the former-day Saints rejoiced that the power of God was theirs, such that by stretching forth their hand in faith it became the hand of the Almighty (see Acts 4:30). Similarly, in a revelation given through the Prophet Joseph Smith to Edward Partridge, "the Lord God, the Mighty One of Israel," said: "I will lay my hand upon you by the hand of my servant Sidney Rigdon, and you shall receive my Spirit, the Holy Ghost, even the Comforter, which shall teach you the peaceable things of the kingdom" (D&C 36:1–2).

As it is with the performance of ordinances, so it is in regard to the working of miracles. Jesus came in his Father's name and in his own right, and when he performed miracles he acted in all the majesty of his own divine calling. He healed the sick and forgave sins; in so doing he illustrated his power over both physical and spiritual maladies (see JST, Matthew 9:1–5; compare JST, Luke 5:23). Jesus is Jehovah, and Jehovah is God, and God works miracles in his own right; he needs neither the name nor the power of another. In contrast, all those who are agents of the Lord act and operate and are authorized by the name above all other names, the name of Jesus Christ (see Ephesians 3:15; Philippians 2:9).

Our Lord and Savior, even as an exalted and resurrected being, continued to pray to his Father, sometimes praying in words of such spiritual grandeur that they could not be repeated or written (see 3 Nephi 17:13–17; 19:31–36). And we are commanded to pattern our prayers after his. Further, we are commanded to pray to the Father in the name of the Son. Our prayers do not go through the Son to the Father, for we are commanded to "come boldly unto the throne of grace" (Hebrews 4:16; compare Moses 7:59). Rather, we are entitled to address the Father directly, because of the Son—because of his ministry of reconciliation, his advocacy of our cause, and his intercession on our behalf (see Alma 33:8–11, 16; D&C 45:3–5). But there is more. We are to pray in the name of Jesus Christ. What does it mean? Is it not the same as with preaching and prophesying and performing ordinances and miracles? All of these are done in his name. When we pray in Christ's name, among other things, we seek to put ourselves in his place and stead. We say the words he would say, because our prayers, when they meet the divine standard, are spoken by the power of the Holy Ghost. And because they are spoken in the name of the blessed Jesus, our words become his words; they are what he would say in the same situation. Truly, "he that asketh in the Spirit asketh according to the will of God; wherefore it is done even as he asketh" (D&C 46:30; see also Helaman 10:5).

Taking the Name of God in Vain

How then do we become guilty of taking the name of God in vain, whether it be the name of the Father or of the Son? Let us first define a few terms. The words that are used in Exodus 20:7 are highly significant. The King James Version has it: "Thou shalt not *take* the name of the Lord thy God in *vain*." The word translated *take* is from the Hebrew word *nasah*, used in several related ways in the Old Testament—to lift or lift up, raise, bear or carry (as we carry a burden), and take or carry away (unjustly). Thus we might speak of taking the name of God in the sense of lifting up or holding up the name, bearing the name of God as we would a standard or a banner, or taking away (from its proper context) the name of God. The word translated *vain* is from the Hebrew word *shav*, meaning empty, worthless, meaningless, even waste and disorder. As one biblical scholar has observed, vain implies "emptiness—a wandering in shadows without substance, a life lived without the possibility of satisfaction." (Lawrence O. Richards, *Expository Dictionary of Bible Words*, p. 608.) What, then, are some ways men and women take the name of God in vain?

1. *Through profanity and vulgarity.* The most commonly understood violation is that of speaking the name of Deity in the context of cursing or profaning. It is interesting to note that the word *profane* means literally (Latin, *profanum*) "outside the temple." What a marvelous way to describe the profanation of the name of God: to take that which is most holy, to remove it from its hallowed setting, and to thrust it into an environment that is unholy and unclean! Thus alternate translations of this passage read as follows: "You must not make wrong use of the name of the

Lord your God" (Revised English Bible); "You shall not make wrongful use of the name of the Lord your God" (New Revised Standard Version); "You shall not misuse the name of the Lord your God" (New International Version). President Gordon B. Hinckley has taught: "So serious was violation of this law considered in ancient Israel that blasphemy of the name of the Lord was regarded as a capital crime. . . . While that most serious of penalties has long since ceased to be inflicted, the gravity of the sin has not changed." (Conference Report, October 1987, p. 56.)

The growing amount of profanity and vulgarity in music, books, television, and the motion picture industry merely serves as a commentary on our times. It just may be that people's inhumanity to people is not unrelated to their neglect of sacred matters, that the growing harshness, crudeness, and insensitivity in society is correlated directly with ignoring, denying, and defying God. Our speech too often betrays us; it shows what and who we are. One who loves the Lord, cherishes his word, and bows beneath his rod seeks always to act and speak with deferential reverence toward Deity. On the other hand, one who knows not God, who finds no personal value in worship or devotion, has no meaningful concept of the holy or of holiness. For such persons there may be no sense of restraint in regard to speech, no hesitation to lift the sacred out of its context and thrust it into the profane.

In a modern revelation, the Lord declared: "Behold, I am from above, and my power lieth beneath. I am over all, and in all, and through all, and search all things, and the day cometh that all things shall be subject unto me. Behold, I am Alpha and Omega, even Jesus Christ. Wherefore, let all men beware how they take my name in their lips—for behold, verily I say, that many there be who are under this condemnation, who use the name of the Lord, and use it in vain, having not authority. . . . Remember that that which cometh from above is sacred, and must be spoken with care, and by constraint of the

Spirit; and in this there is no condemnation." (D&C 63:59–62, 64.)

The Lord is from above, as is his word. When we speak of him or take his name, we should and must do so with the deepest reverence. To do otherwise is to take or hold up or raise up his holy name before others without serious thought, without appropriate reflection, in vain. Elder Dallin H. Oaks thus explained that "we take the name of the Lord in vain when we use his name without authority. This obviously occurs when the sacred names of God the Father and his Son, Jesus Christ, are used in what is called profanity: in hateful cursings, in angry denunciations, or as marks of punctuation in common discourse." On the other hand, Elder Oaks added, "The names of the Father and the Son are used with authority when we reverently teach and testify of them, when we pray, and when we perform the sacred ordinances of the priesthood." (Conference Report, April 1986, p. 66.)

2. *Through the breaking of oaths and covenants.* To ancient Israel the Lord said: "Ye shall not swear by my name falsely, neither shalt thou profane the name of thy God; I am the Lord" (Leviticus 19:12). Thus the Jewish Publication Society translation of Exodus 20:7 is: "You shall not swear falsely by the name of the Lord your God." One commentator has written: "This prohibition applies strictly to perjury or false swearing, the breaking of a promise or contract that has been sealed with an oath in the name of God. He will not allow His name to be associated with any act of falsehood or treachery. His name must not be taken in vain, i.e., lightly or heedlessly." (J. R. Dummelow, *A Commentary on the Holy Bible*, p. 67.) Without truth there can be no society, no order among men and women.

Anciently an oath was a means of impressing the necessity of truth and integrity upon parties to an agreement or upon witnesses in an investigation. That obligation was fortified by holy words and sacred acts intended to bring a sense of confidence and assurance to those involved. Thus the legal procedure, of which an oath was a part, was administered by persons and sealed by the invocation of the name of Deity. To perjure such an oath was indeed a very serious matter and was not to go unpunished (see Ezekiel 17:13, 16, 18–19). In time, people began to abuse the oath, to swear in a manner that was unholy, inappropriate, or that would allow for loopholes. Jesus thus called his followers to a greater accountability: "Swear not at all," he said, "neither by heaven; for it is God's throne: nor by the earth; for it is his footstool: neither by Jerusalem; for it is the city of the great King. Neither shalt thou swear by thy head, because thou canst not make one hair white or black. But let your communication be, Yea, yea; Nay, nay: for whatsoever is more than these cometh of evil." (Matthew 5:34–37.) His was a call to a higher righteousness, a call to his disciples to let their word be their bond. If one says "Yes" as a part of a legal or interpersonal arrangement, then mean "Yes." If one says "No," then mean "No." Personal honor and integrity are at stake.

Covenants are two-way promises between us and our God. All gospel covenants and ordinances are administered and entered into in the name of Jesus Christ. Nothing can be done for the salvation of mankind in any other name or by any other authority. The composite of "all covenants, contracts, bonds, obligations, oaths, vows, performances, connections, associations, or expectations" constitutes the new and everlasting covenant (D&C 132:6–7; compare 1:22; 45:9; 66:2). To willingly or knowingly violate the terms of our covenants or any of the component parts is thus to take the name of the Lord in vain—to take lightly, treat as empty and meaningless, our sacred and solemn obligations. God will not be mocked (Galatians 6:7), nor will he suffer that his holy ordinances are mocked or treated capriciously or cavalierly. The gravity of sin is in proportion to the understanding of the transgressor. Truly, "of him unto whom much is given much is required; and he who sins against the greater light shall receive the greater condemnation" (D&C 82:3; compare 63:66; Luke 12:48). "Hearken and hear, O ye my people, saith the Lord and your God, ye whom I delight to bless with the greatest of all blessings, ye that hear me; and ye that hear me not will I curse, that have professed my name, with the heaviest of all cursings" (D&C 41:1). The Lord has warned that in the last days vengeance will come speedily upon the inhabitants of the earth. "And upon my house shall it begin, and from my house shall it go forth, saith the Lord; first among those among you, saith the Lord, who have professed to know my name and have not known me, and have blasphemed against me in the midst of my house, saith the Lord" (D&C 112:24–26).

3. *Through being flippant, sacrilegious, and irreverent.* The divine decree from Sinai "necessarily forbids all light and irreverent mention of God, or any of his attributes, and . . . we may safely add to all these, that every prayer, . . . etc. that is not accompanied with deep reverence and the genuine spirit of piety is here condemned also." (*Adam Clarke's Commentary on the Bible*, p. 126.)

Several years ago a young man addressed my home ward in sacrament meeting. He said, in essence: "Brothers and sisters, it's great to be in your ward today. I am told that the best way to get a congregation with you is to liven them up with a few jokes." He related several humorous stories, at least a couple of which were inappropriate for the occasion. He then began to do impersonations of the president of the United States, indicating what it would be like if the president were to take the missionary discussions. The congregation roared; at least, some of them did. Some sat in stupor. Others, like myself, wondered what was going on. After fifteen or twenty minutes, the young man looked at his watch and said, "Well, I'd better close now. I say all these things in the name of Jesus Christ. Amen."

His address was amusing, entertaining, something that

might be fun to witness in a roadshow or a youth activity or a family home evening. But we were in a sacrament meeting, one of the sacred worship services of The Church of Jesus Christ of Latter-day Saints. For me there was something haunting about this young man's words, "In the name of Jesus Christ." I had, of course, heard those very words at least ten thousand times over the years. But that day it was different. I became very introspective. I thought of all the times I had delivered talks or offered prayers in the name of Jesus Christ, but had done so without much reflection upon whose name I had taken. I thought of occasions when I had spoken on topics of my own choosing, but topics that may not have represented what the Lord wanted discussed. I thought of those times when I had closed my prayers in a flash, zipping through the name of the Redeemer as though I were sprinting toward some finish line. I thought of the scores of times when I had partaken of the emblems of the body and blood of the Savior with my mind focused on things alien to the spirit of the occasion. It occurred to me then, and has many times since, that one need not be involved with profanity in order to be guilty of taking the name of the Lord our God in vain. He or she needs merely to treat lightly, flippantly, and without serious thought the sobering charge we carry as members of his Church to speak and act in God's name. We are a happy people, and the joy and satisfaction that derive from living the gospel must not be kept a secret. On the other hand, Joseph Smith taught that "the things of God are of deep import; and time, and experience, and careful and ponderous and solemn thoughts can only find them out" (*Teachings of the Prophet Joseph Smith*, p. 137).

As was suggested earlier, our reverence for life—our appreciation for the earth and for all things on its surface, especially human beings—is inextricably tied to our reverence for God. To draw close to Divinity is to come to appreciate man as a divine creation, for "if men do not comprehend the character of God, they do not comprehend themselves" (*Teachings of the Prophet Joseph Smith*, p. 343). Truly, "the nearer a man approaches perfection, the clearer are his views, and the greater his enjoyments" (*Teachings of the Prophet Joseph Smith*, p. 51). People in civilizations that have fallen—whether Greek or Roman or Nephite or Jaredite—often may be characterized as "without order and without mercy," "without principle," and "past feeling" (see Moroni 9:18, 20). On the other hand, those societies that have transcended this fallen world—for example, the righteous societies of old—consisted of peoples who were possessed of great spiritual sensitivity, who were impelled by a desire to attain the holiness God exemplifies, and who reverenced his name and the works of his hands. Having come unto God in the appointed ways, they in time were endowed with the greatest of all fruits of the Spirit: their pure love for God motivated a pure love for their brothers and sisters (see Moroni 7:45–48). They came to be known as Zion—a holy commonwealth where "every man [was] seeking the interest of his neighbor, and doing all things with an eye single to the glory of God" (D&C 82:19).

Praise Ye His Name

To treat God, or that which properly bears his name, with disdain or contempt or even indifference cannot be less than a serious sin. That which profanes the sacred may be born of ignorance, disbelief, or hypocrisy. In any case, it is offensive to the spirit of light and truth; it is attractive to the spirit of darkness and error. Each spirit brings with it its own train of attendants. "That which is of God is light; and he that receiveth light, and continueth in God, receiveth more light; and that light groweth brighter and brighter until the perfect day" (D&C 50:24). Those whose "minds have been darkened [by] unbelief" because they have "treated lightly" the manifestations of heaven are "under condemnation"; unless they repent, theirs is the promise of a scourge and judgment, for they have profaned the sacred (see D&C 84:54–59).

To be called upon to speak or act in the name of God is a sacred trust. It is deserving of solemn and ponderous thought. One wonders if we would not preach more gospel doctrines and bear more fervent testimonies if we had fixed in our minds the weighty fact that the words spoken or the deeds done are not ours alone, but they are the words and actions of our eternal Principal. If we speak or act or pray without seeking inspiration, if we teach for doctrine the views and philosophies of men, if we act or perform anything flippantly or lightly—if we do such things all "in the name of the Lord," one wonders whether we are not taking the name of God in vain. Jesus, as the agent of Elohim, was engaged in his Father's business. We have a like appointment, and our divine commission includes the sobering provision: "Wherefore, as ye are agents, ye are on the Lord's errand; and whatever ye do according to the will of the Lord is the Lord's business" (D&C 64:29). As President Spencer W. Kimball counseled: "It is not enough to refrain from profanity or blasphemy. We need to make important in our lives the name of the Lord. While we do not use the Lord's name lightly, we should not leave our friends or our neighbors or our children in any doubt as to where we stand. Let there be no doubt about our being followers of Jesus Christ." (Conference Report, October 1978, p. 7.) We are counseled by him who is Eternal: "Take upon you the name of Christ, and speak the truth in soberness" (D&C 18:21).

The Lord's people should rejoice in him and sing praises to his holy name continually. When we think of what has been revealed in this day about the Holy One of Israel; when we ponder upon the light and truth and power that have been delivered in this final dispensation of grace; when we reflect upon the fact that living oracles—

Apostles and prophets, special witnesses of the name of Christ—walk the earth today; when we think that holy temples, hallowed edifices upon which God has placed his name and in which the ordinances associated with eventually having the name of God sealed upon our foreheads forever may be received—when we ponder such blessings, our souls should well up with eternal gratitude. Truly our cup is full. Our desires to acknowledge, recognize, and praise him should know no bounds.

With a fervor and zeal born of the Spirit, and one which we might well emulate, the Psalmist proclaimed: "O Lord [Jehovah] our Lord, how excellent is thy name in all the earth! who hast set thy glory above the heavens" (Psalm 8:1). The Apostle Paul counseled the Corinthians: "Know ye not that ye are the temple of God, and that the Spirit of God dwelleth in you? If any man defile the temple of God, him shall God destroy; for the temple of God is holy, which temple ye are." (1 Corinthians 3:16–17; see also 6:19–20.) Being true to what and who we are thus entails embodying a divine principle, a principle that identifies sacred edifices throughout the earth and also identifies the people of God: "Holiness to the Lord."

CHAPTER 3

Christ-Centered Leadership

I am not trained formally in management or organizational behavior, but I have thought much about the matter of leadership, of divine leadership, of what we sometimes call Christ-centered leadership. I have studied the life of the Master. I have studied the lives and teachings of those chosen by him to lead his Church. And I have studied the revelations given through the prophets to guide the Lord's people. From that study, from my own contact with some of the great Christian leaders in our day, and in conjunction with much introspection, I have drawn some tentative conclusions. Though I am painfully aware that in the past, through the power of a pernicious persuasion or personal charisma, some have led others to do evil or to accomplish the forbidden, the leadership of which we shall speak now is righteous leadership, the ability to make a difference for good in the lives of others. Though I do not pretend to originality, I offer the following principles for our consideration.

They Are What They Teach

Christ-centered leaders are the embodiment of their message or philosophy. In short, they practice what they preach. No, that is not strong enough. They *are* what they preach. In this principle, as in all others we will note here, Jesus the Christ stands as the preeminent example. Jesus said: "I am the way, the truth, and the life: no man cometh unto the Father, but by me" (John 14:6). It is not just that the Son of God brought light into a darkened and fallen world; he is the Light (see 3 Nephi 11:11). It is not just that our Savior showed us the way; he is the Way (see John 14:6). It is not just that Christ made the resurrection available; he is the Resurrection (see John 11:25). And it is not just that Jesus of Nazareth restored the truth and taught the truth; he is the Truth (see John 14:6). Our society has inherited a Greek notion of truth, one that emphasizes truth as something to be learned, a matter of the head. In fact, the Hebrew notion of truth was something we *do* and, more precisely, something we *are*, a matter of the heart. We aren't expected to simply know the truth; we are expected to do the truth and be the truth. In short, the Lord expects us to live truthfully.

Just as it is true that "a double minded man is unstable in all his ways" (James 1:8), so a man or woman who attempts to lead others to do X while believing or being Y will be frustrated in the effort. The leader will have the power of presence, the proper power of persuasion, only to the degree that he or she is true to his or her own values. The philosophy that many of us have heard so many times of "Don't do what I do, do what I say to do" is at best a hollow message. On the other hand, people are attracted to and have little difficulty in following someone who is possessed of integrity, someone who stands up for what he or she believes. There is a visible strength to be found in one who is transparent, free of ulterior motives, undivided and focused. From this point of view, people do not become leaders through striving to be leaders; rather, they become leaders through striving to live in harmony with what is right.

They Are Founded on Truth

Christ-centered leaders are built upon a foundation of truth. It is terribly difficult to lead people in a cause or direct their efforts toward an outcome that is untrue or inaccurate or irrelevant. Truth, that which the revelations describe as "knowledge of things as they are, and as they were, and as they are to come" (D&C 93:24), has a power all its own; in the words of Joseph Smith, "Truth will cut its own way" (*Teachings of the Prophet Joseph Smith*, p. 313). And just as there is something curiously attractive about that which is true, so also is there a fascination with one who speaks the truth and operates thereby. Such a person knows the truth and feels the truth. He or she learns to operate and make decisions by principle. Knowing principles and seeing their timelessness, he or she is able to handle myriad situations. President Spencer W. Kimball taught: "Jesus operated from a base of fixed principles or truths rather than making up the rules as he went along. Thus, his leadership style was not only correct, but also constant. So many secular leaders today are like chameleons; they change their hues and views to fit the situation—which only tends to confuse associates and followers who cannot be certain what course is being pursued. Those who cling to power at the expense of principle often end up doing almost anything to perpetuate their power." ("Jesus: The Perfect Leader," p. 5.)

In that same spirit, my observation is that effective leaders have the patience and self-discipline to allow others to function within the parameters of their given assignments and in harmony with the truths set forth by the leader. Few things are quite as frustrating as to work under the direction of a leader who is so intent on *product* that he or she stifles the *process* by seeking to do everyone's job, to make certain that every assignment is carried out in just the way he or she wants it done. This is what might be called "smother leadership," an administrative style that evidences the leader's distrust in co-workers, a style which sooner or later sends those co-workers up the wall.

President Joseph F. Smith spoke of the necessity for patience on the part of those who lead in the Church, a lesson which stretches well beyond the Church. "In leaders," he said, "undue impatience and a gloomy mind are almost unpardonable, and it sometimes takes almost as much courage to wait as to act. It is to be hoped, then, that the leaders of God's people, and the people themselves, will not feel that they must have at once a solution of every question that arises to disturb the even tenor of their way." (*Gospel Doctrine*, p. 156.) President Harold B. Lee was fond of quoting the last two verses of section 107 of the Doctrine and Covenants to make this point. "Therefore *let* every man learn his duty," he often said, placing the appropriate stress on *let* in order to convey the meaning of allow, permit, encourage. He explained: "Let them do everything within their power, and you stand in the background and teach them *how* to do it. I think therein is the secret of growth, to fix responsibility and then teach our people *how to carry* that responsibility." (Cited by N. Eldon Tanner, in "Leading As the Savior Led," p. 6.)

Perhaps it is in that spirit that we ought to consider the now-famous statement attributed to Joseph Smith about governing the people. Elder John Taylor asked: "What is it that will enable one man to govern his fellows aright? It is just as Joseph Smith said to a certain man who asked him, 'How do you govern such a vast people as this?' 'Oh,' says Joseph, 'it is very easy.' 'Why,' says the man, 'but we find it very difficult.' 'But,' said Joseph, 'it is very easy, for I

"Christ Raising the Daughter of Jairus," by Greg K. Olsen.
Courtesy of The Church of Jesus Christ of Latter-day Saints.

"Christ at Pool of Bethesda," by Gary E. Smith.

teach the people correct principles and they govern themselves.'" (*Journal of Discourses* 10:57–58.)

Along the same lines, Elder Erastus Snow stated in 1883: "My experience and observation of the Latter-day Saints is that they are the hardest people I know anything about to either drive or lead in a wrong direction. Brother [George Q.] Cannon speaks of President Young and President Taylor, and other good men, our leaders, being led, as it were, by a hair in obedience to the Priesthood, which implies simply obedience to truth and to correct doctrine, and to righteousness. This is the explanation the Prophet Joseph Smith gave to a certain lawyer in his time who came to see him and his people and expressed astonishment and surprise at the ease with which he controlled the people, and said it was something that was not to be found among the learned men of the world. Said he: 'We cannot do it. What is the secret of your success?' 'Why,' said the Prophet, 'I do not govern the people. I teach them correct principles and they govern themselves.'" (*Journal of Discourses* 24:158–59.) Or, as President Brigham Young put it succinctly, "Teach the people true knowledge, and they will govern themselves" (*Journal of Discourses* 10:190; compare 12:257). This is not simply laissez-faire leadership, not "every man for himself," not "do your own thing." Rather, the leader teaches and builds a foundation of true principles and then allows those who work under his or her direction to govern themselves in accordance with those principles.

They Draw People Through Their Own Goodness

Christ-centered leaders are concerned with more than the shaping of others' behavior and the controlling of their actions. They lead by virtue of who they are, by the power of their person and presence. In the inspired epistle from Liberty Jail, Joseph Smith provided a list of timely and timeless qualities that ought to characterize anyone who seeks to lead in righteousness. They included persuasion, long-suffering, gentleness and meekness, unfeigned love, kindness, pure knowledge (or knowledge from a pure source), appropriate (divinely directed) reproof, charity, and virtue. We note with interest that those who govern in this way, the Lord's way, are blessed with the constant companionship of the Holy Ghost, and that "[their] dominion shall be an everlasting dominion, and without compulsory means it shall flow unto [them] forever and ever" (D&C 121:41–46). To put it simply, one who leads and governs in this manner will have no need to coerce or force or manipulate or manufacture a following; people automatically follow such a person.

A Christian counselor made an important point in this regard. The primary thrust of his message is the importance of being changed "from the inside out," but notice how terribly relevant his remarks are to our discussion.

> One friend comes to mind who is self-disciplined in his health habits. He resists temptation to eat too many sweets, he jogs faithfully, and he paces his workload well. I respect him for that. His behavior reflects a commendable level of willpower, a level that sometimes puts to shame my efforts to eat, exercise, and work properly.
>
> Another friend responds to a terribly disappointing and painful struggle in his life by loving others more deeply. He feels his pain but somehow uses it to make himself more aware of others' pain and of God's ability to encourage. When I look at his life, words like noble, godly, and rich come to mind.
>
> Observing habits of self-discipline, orderliness, and general cordiality do not bring to mind those same words. I describe my well-disciplined friend as effective, respectable, and nice. When I look at his life I think, "I should be more disciplined," I feel a bit pressured, somewhat guilty, and oc-

casionally motivated. The effect of my struggling friend, on the other hand, is *not* to make me say, "I *should* be more disciplined," but "I *want* to be more loving."

The difference is enormous. Some people push me to *do* better by trying harder. Others draw me to *be* better by enticing me with an indefinable quality about their lives that seems to grow out of an unusual relationship with Christ. (Larry Crabb, *Inside Out*, p. 41.)

We are able to lead people only to the degree that we have some place to take them. We are able to lead people only to the degree that our followers or co-workers desire to share our vision of what is to be. In this sense, Christ-centered leadership consists in lifting and building and strengthening others. To quote President Harold B. Lee, "You cannot lift another soul until you are standing on higher ground than he is. You must be sure, if you would rescue the man, that you yourself are setting the example of what you would have him be. You cannot light a fire in another soul unless it is burning in your own soul." (Conference Report, April 1973, p. 178.)

They Point Others to Higher Things

Christ-centered leaders seek to point their followers beyond themselves. Jesus illustrates this principle perfectly. He taught that he came to do his Father's will; that his doctrine was not his but rather the doctrine of Him that sent him; that he did nothing but what he had seen his Father do; and that there was none good but God, his Father. He constantly deferred to the Father and sought with all his heart to turn his followers to the Almighty Elohim. Similarly, John the Baptist knew his place, acknowledged that his Master was greater than he, that he (John) was not worthy to untie the Lord's shoes. In a moment of perfect submission and acknowledgement, John spoke in poignant praise of the Savior: "He must increase, but I must decrease" (John 3:30).

Christ is God. He is the Lord Omnipotent. It is appropriate and right, therefore, for him to encourage others to come unto the Father in his name and be saved. We worship Jesus Christ in that we seek to be like him, to think and act and be as he is. We seek with all our souls to be counted worthy to be called disciples of the Christ. Emulation and imitation are thus the highest forms of devotion to him. In this he stands alone. No other being who has ever lived on this earth—no matter the depth of his commitment or the breadth of her integrity and goodness—is deserving of that kind of discipleship. In that spirit, the Christ-centered leader seeks to assist others to move closer to the divine. In the Church we would say that such a leader has an eye single to the glory of God. He knows full well that he is not the light; the Lord is the light. She is a lamp at best, a dim and lesser reflection of the greater. Service and leadership that are self-serving or that focus attention on the leader fall short of the divine standard. The leader has not succeeded if the followers or co-workers are merely wowed or awed by their leader. President David O. McKay pointed out:

> In the realm of personality, and in the kingdom of character, Christ was supreme. By personality, I mean all that may be included in individuality. Personality is a gift from God; it is indeed a "pearl of great price," an eternal blessing.
>
> Fellow workers, you and I cannot hope to exert even to a small degree the personality of our great teacher, Jesus Christ. Each one's personality may be compared to the Savior's personality only as one little sunbeam to the mighty sun itself; and yet, though infinitely less in degree, each leader's, each teacher's personality should be the same in kind. In the realm of character, each leader and teacher may be superior, and such a magnet as to draw around him or

her, in an indescribable way, those whom he or she would lead or teach. It is the radiation of the light that attracts.

However, no matter how attractive the personality may be, that leader or teacher fails in the work assigned if the leader or teacher directs the love of the member only to the personality of the leader or teacher. (Conference Report, October 1968, p. 143.)

It has been my experience also that since the Christ-centered leader is not in the business to build a following, since there are some difficult matters which require moral courage and individual strength, there will always be moments of loneliness and alienation. It is not easy to stand up for what is right, especially when a different approach to the issue would result in accolades and praise. Elder Gordon B. Hinckley, in speaking to BYU students in 1969, said some things which have remarkable relevance many years after they were spoken:

> There is a great loneliness in leadership, but . . . we have to live with ourselves. A man has to live with his conscience. . . .
>
> There is a loneliness in all aspects of leadership. I think we feel it somewhat in this University. BYU is being discussed across the nation today because of some of our practices and some of our policies and some of our procedures, but I would like to offer the thought that no institution and no man ever lived at peace with itself or with himself in a spirit of compromise. We have to stand for the policy that we have adopted. We may wonder in our hearts, but we have to stand on that position set for us by him who leads us, our Prophet.
>
> It was ever thus. The price of leadership is loneliness. The price of adherence to conscience is loneliness. The price of adherence to principle is loneliness. I think it is inescapable. The Savior of the world was a man who walked in loneliness. (*The Loneliness of Leadership*, p. 3.)

They Love Those They Serve

Christ-centered leaders love those they are appointed to lead. Though it is true that the effective leader knows and feels and operates according to truth, for the leader who walks in the shadow of the Master there is a burning realization that people are more important than abstract truth. Let me say that again: People are more important than abstract truth. Twenty years ago I would have recoiled in response to such a bold declaration with, "Oh no. Nothing is more important than truth!" I know better now. To the degree that I as a leader am so bent on accomplishments; to the degree that I as a leader am so riveted on goal attainment and product that I tend to trample on or treat lightly the feelings of those with whom I work, I have failed. God himself is in the business of people (Moses 1:39), and so must we be. People are his most important product. It must be so with us.

I have worked under the direction of managers whose intensity constantly affirmed our fear that we as subordinates were at best cogs in a wheel, means to some greater end. I have witnessed firsthand the discouragement in the eyes and hearts of those who sense that they matter only to the extent that they contribute to the production of some thing. On the other hand, it has been my privilege to work closely with highly effective leaders (in and out of the Church), men and women who do their jobs superbly well, but whose sense of balance and whose sensitivity to others have caused me to marvel. They are truly most successful who are able to focus appropriately on the task to be done, but to do so with a humaneness and a sincerity that radiates care and concern for people. Joseph Smith the Prophet remarked: "Sectarian priests cry out concerning me, and ask, 'Why is it this babbler gains so many followers, and retains them?' I answer, It is because I possess the principle of love. All I can offer the world is a good heart and a good hand." (*Teachings of the Prophet*

Joseph Smith, p. 313.) People don't want mushy sentimentality; they want concern. Most people don't want to be coddled; they want to be treated with respect and consideration. And they want to feel that they are as important as some computer printout or statistical coefficient. And they deserve to feel that way. In this sense, empathy is at least as important as efficiency.

They Lead by Teaching

For me, leadership is a lot like teaching. There are things associated with effective and inspirational teaching that are simply not programmable, not reducible to formulae, lists, and behavior modification. The ability to teach the gospel with power and persuasion is a gift of the Spirit. It is something which is divinely bestowed. To some degree I feel that leadership is much the same. There are definite things we can do to improve our organizational abilities, better utilize our time, talents, and resources, and focus ourselves and our co-workers more completely on the task ahead. But then there is that indefinable quality, that spark, that light, that intangible something that characterizes the leader and that always seems to make a difference for good in the lives of others.

Those who believe in God, who acknowledge the power of the Almighty in transforming people and circumstances, would do well to seek divine guidance and assistance in leading others. Joseph Smith offered profound counsel to the Saints on leading people toward righteous ends, counsel which should have obvious relevance for all aspects of leadership: "Thy mind, O man! if thou wilt lead a soul unto salvation, must stretch as high as the utmost heavens, and search into and contemplate the darkest abyss, and the broad expanse of eternity—thou must commune with God. How much more dignified and noble are the thoughts of God, than the vain imaginations of the human heart! None but fools will trifle with the souls of men." (*Teachings of the Prophet Joseph Smith*, p. 137.)

And so for me a leader is a teacher. It is not enough to be a great manager, a workaholic, or a clever executive. A leader is a teacher. It would never seem appropriate to call Jesus an executive or a personnel director or a manager. He was a teacher. In fact, he was and is the great Teacher. And surely no one has led people or overthrown inequity or established goodness in the earth like Jesus and those who have ministered in his name and followed his example.

Conclusion

There is a crying need for leadership in today's world, particularly leadership that is Christ-centered. Many of us will serve in positions of responsibility in the Church and will thus be in a position to teach people according to the covenants. Others of us will be in positions of responsibility in which we are prevented from articulating directly the principles of the gospel. Wherever we work, however, we can live and be what the Christ would have us be; wherever we are we can stand for truth and stand up for people.

In November 1975, Charles H. Malik, professor of Philosophy at American University in Beirut, Lebanon, and former president of the United Nations General Assembly, delivered a forum address at Brigham Young University. To conclude, I quote from a portion of his address.

> I respect all men, and it is from disrespect for none that I say there are no great leaders in the world today. In fact, greatness itself is laughed to scorn. You should not be great today—you should sink yourself into the herd, you should not be distinguished from the crowd, you should simply be one of the many.

The commanding voice is lacking. The voice which speaks little, but which when it speaks, speaks with compelling moral authority—this kind of voice is not congenial to this age. The age flattens and levels down every distinction into drab uniformity. Respect for the high, the noble, the great, the rare, the specimen that appears once every hundred or every thousand years, is gone. Respect at all is gone! If you ask whom and what people do respect, the answer is literally nobody and nothing. This is simply an unrespecting age—it is the age of utter mediocrity. To become a leader today, even a mediocre leader, is a most uphill struggle. You are constantly and in every way and from every side pulled down. One wonders who of those living today will be remembered a thousand years from now—the way we remember with such profound respect Plato, and Aristotle, and Christ, and Paul, and Augustine, and Aquinas.

If you believe in prayer, my friends, and I know you do, then pray that God send great leaders, especially great leaders of the spirit.

A great leader suffers in a hundred different ways, and keeps his suffering to himself.

A great leader survives both his suffering and the fact that nobody knows anything about it.

A great leader loves being alone with God.

A great leader communes with the deepest the ages have known.

A great leader knows there is a higher and there is a lower, and he always seeks the higher, and indeed the highest.

A great leader fights against the spiritual forces of darkness and disintegration, both in his own soul and in the world.

A great leader overcomes himself, rises above himself, daily, minutely.

A great leader is very polite, but he never tones down the truth just to please others.

A great leader never seeks fanfare and publicity—they come to him, and often he rejects them.

A great leader never craves the approval of the world—in fact he often intentionally provokes its disapproval.

A great leader hitches his wagon to the remote, the unattainable, the stars.

A great leader does not worship quantity, multiplicity, perpetual motion—he stubbornly sticks to the one or at most two ultimate truths that there are.

A great leader is very simple, but the moral force of his conviction shines through every tone of his voice and every gesture of his hand.

A great leader lets the oneness of his interest burst forth with endless creativity.

A great leader is absolutely fearless—fearless because he fears only God.

A great leader loves, not sentimentally, not by making an effort, but with the effortless overflow of God's love for him.

A great leader identifies himself with, and is not ashamed of, the deepest in his own tradition.

A great leader is never disturbed by the fact that other traditions too have their own deepest.

A great leader is decisive, yet with the utmost tentativeness and tenderness.

A great leader, under God, does not care if he is crucified—there is something he knows and sees in the distance infinitely more important than to avoid crucifixion.

A great leader knows what the Bible calls "the fulness of the time," I mean the time in which he lives, and God gives him the grace and the power to fulfill that fulness.

You insult a great leader if you call him great; he does not want your judgment; he wants only to please God.

A great leader calls forth the most secret and the most sacred impulses of those whom he leads.

A great leader leads those who are not even aware that they follow him, but only rejoice in the fact that he leads them.

A great leader is at the forefront of danger, be it physical or moral danger, when danger strikes.

A great leader heals.

And so I say, my friends, if you believe in prayer, and I know you do, then pray that God send great leaders, for that is the world's greatest need. (Charles H. Malik, forum address, pp. 543–45; see also Malik, "Leadership," pp. 8–9.)

My hope is for the development of good people, people whose eyes are single to the glory of God, people whose hearts are fastened to righteousness and truth, people who love people, people who seek to lead as he does who is our Good Shepherd. If we can raise up a generation of righteous men and women, we shall have sufficient leadership to meet the challenges ahead.

CHAPTER 4

Christ-Centered Love

T here seems to be one thing about which Christians around the globe agree in regard to Jesus of Nazareth. They may disagree as to whether he was born of a virgin, healed the sick and raised the dead, died and rose again from the tomb. They may debate whether he was indeed God. But most agree—at least those who accept the accounts of his life and ministry in the Gospels—that he loved people, that he was the embodiment of compassion and empathy. Jesus loved. He was in the business of people.

Love Waxes Cold

Our Lord warned that in a day when iniquity would abound, the love of many would wax cold (see D&C 45:27; Joseph Smith—Matthew 1:10, 30). Love is a priceless virtue, a heavenly quality, but it can survive only in the heart of one who is attempting to be true to what he or she knows to be right. To sin against light is to open the door to darkness and to close the door on those divine refinements that make men and women men and women.

One of the harsh realities that is highlighted by the immorality of our own day is that sexual expression without the commitment, dedication, and devotion associated with love leads to estrangement. Writing with the perspective of thousands of years before them, Will and Ariel Durant observed: "No one man, however brilliant or well-informed, can come in one lifetime to such fullness of understanding as to safely judge and dismiss the customs and institutions of his society, for these are the wisdom of generations after centuries of experiment in the laboratory of history. A youth boiling with hormones will wonder why he should not give full freedom to his sexual desires; and if he is unchecked by custom, morals, or laws, he may ruin his life before he matures sufficiently to understand that sex is a river of fire that must be banked and cooled by a hundred restraints if it is not to consume in chaos both the individual and the group." (*The Lessons of History*, pp. 35–36.)

In my mind, no scriptural narrative more poignantly portrays the tragedy and heartbreak and estrangement that flow freely in the wake of sexual sin than the story of Amnon, son of David. The scriptures affirm through myriad examples that the sins of the fathers—through behavioral patterns and lifestyles—are indeed answered upon the heads of the children. And so it was with the family of David. David, the man who was after the Lord's own heart; David, the man who united all Israel into one empire; even this David fell from grace through yielding to the allurements of the flesh.

David's son Amnon was a man whose judgment became clouded by his passions. His lust for his step-sister Tamar was such that he and a friend devised a nefarious plan to allow Amnon to achieve a sexual conquest over

the young woman. Feigning illness, Amnon requested
that Tamar be sent to him with food. "And when she had
brought them unto him to eat, he took hold of her, and
said unto her, Come lie with me, my sister. And she answered him, Nay, my brother, do not force me; for no such
thing ought to be done in Israel: do not thou this folly."
And now note the pathos but the perspective in her plead-
ings: "And I, whither shall I cause my shame to go? and as
for thee, thou shalt be as one of the fools in Israel. Now
therefore, I pray thee, speak unto the king [meaning their
father, David]; for he will not withhold me from thee.
Howbeit he would not hearken unto her voice: but, being
stronger than she, forced her, and lay with her."

And now the clincher, the punchline, the lesson of the
ages: "Then Amnon hated her exceedingly; so that the hatred wherewith he hated her was greater than the love
wherewith he had loved her. And Amnon said unto her,
Arise, be gone." (2 Samuel 13:1–15.)

One can begin to understand why it is that Alma counseled Shiblon, "See that ye bridle all your passions, that ye
may be filled with love" (Alma 38:12). Truly, "God is love;
and he that dwelleth in love dwelleth in God, and God in
him" (1 John 4:16). Lust leads to loneliness. For one who
has received the gospel, unbridled passions are followed
by fear. "He that looketh on a woman to lust after her, or if
any shall commit adultery in their hearts, they shall not
have the Spirit, but shall deny the faith and shall fear"
(D&C 63:16). Fear. Fear of being found out, fear of rejec-
tion, fear of coming face to face with the vainness of one's
own life. On the other hand, one filled with the love of
Christ does not waste his life in worry or ache with anxiety concerning the future. The love of Christ brings peace
and contentment. It settles the soul, rests the road-weary,
and consoles the bereaved. As John taught, "There is no
fear in love; but perfect love casteth out fear" (1 John 4:18;
compare Moroni 8:16).

It is a sad commentary of our time that the refusal to

abide by the divine standards of morality has led to much unhappiness and abuse. Such doings testify that the love of God, given as a free gift through his Son Jesus Christ, has begun to wax cold and thus to wane in the hearts of earth's pilgrims. Wickedness weakens love. Surely if god-like love is a heavenly endowment, then reveling in sin prevents one from receiving and extending such love. Sexual immorality, for example, prostitutes those God-given powers that are so intimately connected with the fountains of human life. Lust is a pitiful substitute for that love which is pure, that expression and that commitment which bind and seal through time and eternity.

I remember all too well what happened to a very close friend of mine many years ago. She began to date a young man who was a member of the Church but whose commitment to the faith was at best marginal. Their time together increased, the moments spent with others decreased, and they were eventually over their heads in a relationship that was forced to ripen before its time. They were married by a justice of the peace and supposed that their dreams had finally come true.

Those dreams were transformed into nightmares in a very short time. I saw the girl several weeks after the marriage. Her face was bruised, her lips were swollen. I asked what had happened. She answered: "He beats me. He doesn't trust me. He follows me everywhere I go. He demands to know where I am every minute of the day. He says to me: 'If you were immoral with me, you'll do the same with anyone else.'"

My heart ached for my friend. The pain in her eyes bespoke a lesson I shall never forget: Righteousness begets trust and understanding and latitude, while sin sires suspicion and alienation and confinement. God's ways expand the soul, while the ways of the world contract the human heart.

The increase of spouse and child abuse, abortion, and sexual deviancy, even among some members of the Church, evidences the painful reality that men and women have not learned to bridle their passions or control their thoughts. Ours is not a moral society, but I know that it is possible to live a moral life in the midst of great sin. It is a challenge, to be sure, but it is possible. God has called upon those of us in the household of faith to stand aloof from the sins of this world. We do so as we avoid, as we would a plague (for surely it is), the videos, the motion pictures, the television programs, the music, and the literature that stifle spiritual sensitivity and deaden those holy emotions and attributes that have always characterized the Lord's people. We are called to a life of holiness. We are called to be a light to a world that wanders in darkness.

As members of The Church of Jesus Christ of Latter-day Saints, those who have received the gift of the Holy Ghost, we are entitled to that purifying and sanctifying influence that heightens our perspective on life and deepens our love for God and his children. Surely people who know where they come from, why they are here in mortality, and where they are going after death can view the world and its inhabitants with a compassion and a concern that few others can fathom; surely those who have by covenant come out of the world unto Christ can seek and eventually embody that love and gentility of soul that are central to the nature of our Master. Ours is a great opportunity to be a leavening influence in the earth, to become as oil on troubled waters. Like salt, however, our influence is direct and lasting only to the degree that we have not lost our savor through mixture and contamination. The love of the Lord can shine through us to a lonely and befuddled world only as we have allowed ourselves to become pure receptacles.

More Precious Than Knowledge

If I were totally honest I would admit that twenty years ago Church talks about love basically turned me off.

I thought it was a rather mushy subject, a topic that was sweet, to be sure, but one that was less than worthy of the time of the Saints. Why, I reasoned, we might as well talk about flowers or sunsets or lovely landscapes. It was sort of a given in my mind that people ought to love one another, so it seemed something that ought to be confined to the slogans or pep talks of the Rotary Club or service organizations. Doctrine was what I demanded; theology was my thing.

Well, I still love to discuss the doctrines of the gospel and find great fulfillment in doing so. I still believe the time in the sacred meetings of the Church is precious and should only be taken up in substantive matters, in saving truths worthy of the blood of Jesus Christ. But a few things have changed in my life, things that tend now to focus my attention not only on God's revelations but also on his ultimate creation—his children.

I have met many noble sons and daughters of God who may not be able to explain properly the doctrine of the Atonement but who nonetheless have the image of Christ in their countenances. I have become acquainted with men and women who constitute that vast body of souls we know as the rank and file of the Church, who by divine standards embody gospel greatness. Many of these choice individuals have lived lives of quiet goodness. Their righteousness is unpretentious, their service spontaneous, unpremeditated, and silent. They are not immune from life's challenges; they agonize over children who stray, they wrestle with personal weaknesses. But they love as the Lord loves.

Their lives bring to mind the story Luke told of a woman—a sinner by some persons' self-righteous standards—who washed Jesus' feet with her tears, wiped his feet with her hair, and anointed them with ointment. Responding to the thoughts of those who prejudged her and were incensed that the Master would allow such a person to minister to him, Jesus said: "Her sins, which are many, are forgiven; for she loved much: but to whom little is forgiven, the same loveth little. And he said unto her, Thy sins are forgiven. . . . Thy faith hath saved thee; go in peace." (Luke 7:37–50.)

As my own soul has been wrenched and stretched by the painful strugglings of this life, as I have wept and prayed and sorrowed for my own sins and those of my loved ones, as my hardened heart has been broken and my spirit crushed under the weight of some of the ironies of this existence, I have come to appreciate with certainty that some things matter even more than what we know does. I have come to believe that feelings are fundamental, that people matter more than anything, that people's feelings are sacred. I have a witness that God expects me to be kindly and gentle to his little ones, whether infant or aged.

Some years ago Elder Jeffrey R. Holland, then president of Brigham Young University, said something about the marriage relationship that went straight to the core of my being. I knew then that it was true and that I was under obligation to conform to its implications. The message reaches well beyond the attitudes and actions of husbands and wives.

> To give ourselves so totally to another person is the most trusting and perhaps the most fateful step we take in life. It seems such a risk and such an act of faith. None of us moving toward the altar would seem to have the confidence to reveal *everything* that we are—all our hopes, all our fears, all our dreams, all our weaknesses—to another person. Safety and good sense and this world's experience suggest that we hang back a little, that we not wear our heart on our sleeve where it can so easily be hurt by one who knows so much about us. We fear, as Zechariah prophesied of Christ, that we will be "wounded in the house of [our] friends." (Zechariah 13:6.)
>
> . . . Pat and I have lived together for [many] years. . . . I may not know everything about her, but I know [many]

years' worth, and she knows that much of me. I know her likes and dislikes, and she knows mine. I know her tastes and interests and hopes and dreams, and she knows mine. As our love has grown and our relationship matured, we have been increasingly open with each other about all of that for [those] years now, and the result is that I know much more clearly how to help her and I know exactly how to hurt her. I may not know all the buttons to push, but I know most of them. And surely God will hold me accountable for any pain I cause her by intentionally pushing the hurtful ones when she has been so trusting of me. To toy with such a sacred trust—her body, her spirit, and her eternal future—and exploit those for my gain, even if only emotional gain, should disqualify me to be her husband and ought to consign my miserable soul to hell. To be that selfish would mean that I am a legal, live-in roomate who shares her company but I am not her husband in any Christian sense of that word. I have not been as Christ is to the church. (*However Long and Hard the Road*, pp. 107–9.)

It just may be that the Keeper of the gate will not be as interested in what we know at the great day of judgment as he will in what we have become. Our mortal medals and our temporal acquisitions may prove to be far less significant in the eternal scheme of things than the enduring personal relationships we have developed and nurtured. Holy writ attests to the fact that the depth of our conversion is and should be reflected in the way we view and treat one another. The Apostle John wrote: "Beloved, let us love one another: for love is of God; and every one that loveth is born of God, and knoweth God" (1 John 4:7). Elder Marvin J. Ashton pointed out that "the way we treat each other is the foundation of the gospel of Jesus Christ." Further, "When we truly become converted to Jesus Christ, committed to Him, an interesting thing happens: our attention turns to the welfare of our fellowmen, and the way we treat others becomes increasingly filled with patience, kindness, a gentle acceptance, and a desire to play a positive role in their lives. This is the beginning of true conversion." (Conference Report, April 1992, pp. 25, 26.)

Not of This World

To love and be loved is a glorious thing, especially in a world where in recent years men's and women's hearts have grown cold. I have come to know that the love of God—what the scriptures denominate as charity, the pure love of Christ (Moroni 7:47)—is not of this world. It is not man-made, and it cannot be manufactured. It is not something that can be programmed. It is of God. It is bestowed by him. I have had a few experiences with this divine principle that attest to its power and influence for good. I share a couple of them here, hoping that what I have learned may be of benefit to someone.

In the mid-1970s, as a seminary instructor I was assigned to teach the Old Testament to six classes of high school students. Having grown up in Louisiana, I had never had the opportunity to enjoy seminary or institute programs, so I was ignorant about what this new experience would entail. As I lay in bed at night during the weeks prior to the start of school, I had marvelous visions of what lay ahead. I could picture myself walking into the classroom, Wilford Woodruff-like, teaching and expounding with great power, watching as young hearts and minds exploded with new insights and expanded with feelings of testimony and conversion.

To say that this was not exactly the experience I did have would be to utter the grossest of understatements. It was a mess! Those kids could not have cared less about what I had to say. I remember quitting every afternoon, only to have my principal and my wife bind up my wounds, paste me back together, and send me back into the arena the next morning. Each night my prayers would go something like this: "Heavenly Father, please bless these irreverent and irresponsible little creatures that they will sense that what I have to say is important. Help them want to be quiet and listen to my lessons."

There was something about the pounding I took each day, however, that began to humble me and force me to pray with greater intensity and deeper earnestness. One night, at what seemed to me to be the point at which I was simply up against the wall, naked in my inabilities and shorn of duplicity and pride, I found myself saying something like the following in prayer: "O Lord, thy servants the prophets have told us that these young people are precious in thy sight and that they have been reserved to come to earth in the Saturday night of time, in a day of great challenge and wickedness. I feel greatly inadequate to accomplish what needs to be done. They need to be prepared, to be taught the gospel. But I am weak and frail, and my feelings for them are not as they should be. Forgive me. Purify my heart and my affections. Make me worthy to teach the youth of the Church."

I do not remember feeling anything at the moment that was unusual, except that sweet peace that comes when we have offered our all to the Lord and presented our petitions to him in sincerity. I walked into my first class the next morning prepared for the typical struggle. The devotional was presented and the prayer was said. I remember very well sitting atop one of the desks and looking out at the class. And then, something happened. Something totally unexpected. I no longer saw these young people in the same way. As I looked into their eyes, there came into my heart an overwhelming feeling of love, a desire to reach out and lift and embrace each and every one of them. For some moments I was unable to speak, only to look at them and feel what I did. I remember that the first words I spoke were these: "I wish I could tell you what I feel."

And then the real miracle took place. One of the students, with much emotion, said: "Brother Millet, we understand. We know what you feel." I wept for a moment as I sat there and shared with them how much I loved them, how much I loved the Lord and his gospel, and how very much I wanted to share with them what I felt in my soul to be true and important. These feelings persisted throughout the day; and within a very short time there were no discipline problems to speak of. The Lord of Love had worked in his mysterious way and had accomplished a great wonder. It was the miracle of love that transformed me and a group of adolescents, that taught us a lasting lesson for life.

I had another experience several years ago that has left its imprint on my soul. My wife, Shauna, received word from some of her friends from high school days that her class would be holding a twentieth-year reunion in August. She was excited to go and be a part of it. She asked me if I would be willing to go with her, so I dutifully smiled and said it sounded like a lot of fun. (To be honest, I couldn't think of anything that might be more deadly than spending five or six hours with a group of people I didn't know from Adam and Eve!)

The plans went forward and the long-anticipated day came. The evening was all I had sensed it would be. My wife is a very loving person and has been so forever, so she has loads of friends. She shook hands and hugged and greeted people with excitement for hours. Once in a while she would say to me: "Bob, could you wait here for just a second? I'll be right back. I want to go over and say something to Brenda (or Bill or Becky)." And so I would stand there, not so patiently, mentally wringing my hands, wondering why time seemed to stand still.

During one of those occasions, at about nine o'clock, I began to feel some bitterness toward my wife for leaving me alone. And then something happened. Something unexpected. I began to be taught and chastened through the medium of memory. I began to sense things I had never sensed before, such as how very much my wife had given of herself to stand by me for so long, to bear and basically rear the children, and to move forward through terribly challenging years without complaint. I reflected with much pain about how often I had been the center of attention, how often I had been the one to win the accolades, while she quietly and in the background went about the task of supporting and sustaining. I pondered in much anguish of soul on the times when I had been insensitive or just plain uncaring. I don't think I am a mean and vicious person by nature, but I suddenly remembered all the times through the years when I had failed to call home and indicate I would be late for dinner, all the times when in the name of physical exhaustion I had failed to assume my part of the parental obligation, and, most painful of all, the occasions when I knew she needed to be alone, to rest, to have time to herself, but when I had elected to do something other than be thoughtful. I didn't have much to say during the rest of the evening, though I tried to act interested in what was going on.

Worrying that perhaps I was not having a glorious time, Shauna eventually suggested that we go home. I nodded. As we drove away, few words were spoken. At a certain point on the way home she turned to me and said sweetly, "I'm so grateful for my life." I was moved to tears but refrained from saying anything. Shauna has the capacity to sit down and go to sleep in one motion, and so we were only home for a few minutes before she dropped off to sleep.

It was after a restless night of facing up to who and what I had been, after a sleepless period of hours with time spent on my knees begging for forgiveness and promising to be better, that I awoke to a new view of things. Sparing the details, let me say simply that without warning I was endowed with a depth of love and caring and affection that was beyond anything earthly. For a period of days I was consumed with charity, the pure love of Christ. With all my soul I loved my wife, my children, and, above all, the Lord and his work. For three days I saw things as they really are.

There is no way for me to describe the immersion into the heavenly element and the tenderness of feelings that accompanied what I can only label as a rebirth. I sang the hymns of Zion with a gusto and an emotion that I had never known. I read the scriptures with different eyes and attended to "new writing" everywhere. I prayed with real intent and with a sense of purpose that had seldom accompanied my petitions before. At the end of a glorious Sabbath day, as Shauna and I stood on our front porch on that breezy August evening, I turned to her, and from the depths of my heart I said: "For reasons that I do not understand, I have been given what I think to be a foretaste of eternal life. If this is what it is like to dwell in the celestial kingdom with God, with my family, and among the Saints, then I will give everything, even my own life, to feel this forever."

Conclusion

Though I have not felt the same intensity of love since that time, except in flashes, the sobering and sacred memory and its effects linger. Nothing is quite the same to me now. I know, to some degree at least, what Nephi meant when he said that he had been filled with God's love, even to the consuming of his flesh (2 Nephi 4:21). I know what Mormon meant when he spoke of the pure love of Christ not alone as the motivation for acts of Christian service but, more important, as the means by which men and women are purified from sin and thereby become the sons and daughters of God (Moroni 7:48). The scriptures teach that we do not come to love as the Lord loves merely because we work hard at it. It is true that we must serve others, that we must concern ourselves with others' needs more than with our own. But that service and that outreach cannot have lasting effect, nor can it result in quiet peace and rest in the giver, unless and until it is motivated from on high.

We must ask for charity. We must plead for it. We must pray, as Mormon counseled, with all the energy of heart, that we might have it bestowed upon us (see Moroni 7:48). As we do so, there will come moments of surpassing import, sublime moments, moments in which we know that what we are feeling for God and his children is akin to what God feels for us. This Christ-centered love soothes and settles the hearts of individuals. It provides moral courage to those who must face difficult challenges. It unites and seals husbands, wives, and children, and grants them a foretaste of heaven. It welds quorums and classes and wards and stakes into a union that is the foundation for Zion, the society of the pure in heart. And, once again, it comes from that Lord who is the source of all that is godlike.

It is thus to Jesus Christ that we look—in this endeavor, as in all other righteous efforts—to obtain charity, "the highest pinnacle the human soul can reach and the deepest expression of the human heart" (Howard W. Hunter, Conference Report, April 1992, p. 85). And, as the Apostle Paul testified, there is a sacred sealing, a binding tie associated with that love. "I am persuaded," he wrote to the Romans, "that neither death, nor life, nor angels, nor principalities, nor powers, nor things present, nor things to come, nor height, nor depth, nor any other creature, shall be able to separate us from the love of God, which is in Christ Jesus our Lord" (Romans 8:38–39).

CHAPTER 5

The Christian's Descent into Glory

One of the realities of Christian discipleship is that a person must go down in order to come up. That is, the path to glory is a downward path, a route that leads necessarily through pain and heartache and awful irony. After having transgressed in Eden, Adam and Eve were prevented from partaking of the fruit of the tree of life. They were required to pass through mortality before they would be prepared for immortality, to descend to the depths before they could ascend to the majesty of celestial life. And so it is with all of us.

The Call to Condescend

Nephi was given a vision of the condescension of God (see 1 Nephi 11). Having seen first that a mortal woman

would bring forth a son—the Only Begotten Son of God—
fathered by the Almighty Elohim, Nephi witnessed the
condescension of God the Son: the coming to earth of
Jehovah, the descent into mortality of the Lord Omnipotent. Indeed, the son of Lehi became privy to a powerful
message—that only through such condescension could the
consummation of the great plan of happiness be brought
to pass. The God of our fathers was required to descend
below all things in order to be able to ascend to celestial
heights, and, further, in order for the posterity of Adam
and Eve to enjoy the same potential.

The Apostle Paul described Christ's descent below all
things as follows: "Let this mind be in you, which was also
in Christ Jesus: who, being in the form of God, thought it
not robbery to be equal with God: but made himself of no
reputation, and took upon him the form of a servant, and
was made in the likeness of men: and being found in
fashion as a man, he humbled himself, and became obedient unto death, even the death of the cross. Wherefore
God also hath highly exalted him, and given him a name
which is above every name." (Philippians 2:5–9.) As Paul
said elsewhere: "Ye know the grace of our Lord Jesus
Christ, that, though he was rich, yet for your sakes he became poor, that ye through his poverty might be rich" (2
Corinthians 8:9). Also: "He that descended [into the lower
parts of the earth] is the same also that ascended up far
above all heavens, that he might fill all things." (Ephesians
4:9–10.)

Jesus was spared no agony. There was no pain, no suffering, no loneliness or alienation he could escape, no
bitter draught he was not required to imbibe. In
Gethsemane and on Golgotha he truly descended below
all things that he might comprehend all things (see D&C
88:6) and that thereby his empathy for all men and women
might be perfected (see Alma 7:11–13). Jesus trod the
winepress alone and was thus subject to "the fierceness of
the wrath of Almighty God" (see Isaiah 63:3; D&C 76:107;

88:106; 133:50), the withdrawal of the Father's strengthening Spirit. He suffered more than man (meaning mortal man, unaided by divine influence) can suffer (see Mosiah 3:7). Truly, as Joseph Smith explained, Jesus Christ "descended in suffering below that which man can suffer; or, in other words, suffered greater sufferings, and was exposed to more powerful contradictions than any man can be." (*Lectures on Faith* 5:2; compare Hebrews 12:3.)

Two Christian co-authors have observed: "Once His life on earth began, Jesus never stopped descending. Omnipotent, He cried; the owner of all things, He had no home. The King of Kings, He became a bondservant; the source of truth, He was found guilty of blasphemy; the Creator, He was spit on by the creatures; the giver of life, He was crucified naked on a cross—bleeding, gasping for air. With His death, the descent was complete—from the pinnacle of praise in the universe to the ultimate debasement and torture of death on a cross, the innocent victim of human wickedness." (Bill Hybels and Rob Wilkins, *Descending into Greatness*, pp. 18–19.)

And what of this suffering and death? What of this condescension? We know it was necessary in order for the infinite atoning sacrifice to be accomplished, but is there more? Is such a thing expected of *us*? Of course, we are in no position to suffer and bleed and die for others' sins and infirmities. Of course, we cannot die and raise ourselves from the tomb and thereby open the door to immortality, as did our Master. Jesus was and is the only Savior of mankind. But is there a pattern, a type, in his condescension that has direct application to our lives?

The call of Christ is a call to be *downwardly mobile*. This is "not just a matter of how much money we give away, but how much of ourselves we yield, how much of the sin and excess in our lives we are willing to tear away. It is an attitude marked by strength of character. And we do not grow in character without pain." (Hybels and Wilkins, *Descending into Greatness*, p. 66.) The challenge to live in

the world without being of the world is the challenge of
seeing to it that our attachments, our values, and our loy-
alties are not determined or driven by telestial things. The
fleeting and the ephemeral must not obsess us. In reality, it
is not the case that the one who leaves this world having
acquired the most toys wins in the game of life. The
Christian call to downward mobility is not necessarily the
call to failure or obscurity, but our covenant with Christ
must be secure enough in our souls that we would be
willing to be judged a failure (by this world's standards)
or willing to be excluded from the chief seats in the secular
synagogues if faithfulness to principle required it. Truly,
down is the only way up.

The Call to Lose

We live in a world where winning is everything. In our
society there are few rewards for second place. We are
taught from childhood the absolute necessity of excelling,
of being the best in the class, the finest on the block, the
most successful in the industry. Too often there develops
in time within the will of the achiever a competitive spirit
that can drive out cooperation, consideration, and compassion. Product becomes more prized than process, and
eventually more sacred than people. While Christ calls
upon us to yield, the world beckons us to seek power.
"Let's be honest. Doesn't the world's way make more
sense? . . . If we gather enough power, we need rely only
on ourselves. Trust becomes a matter of the size of our bi-
ceps or our B2s, or whatever else we use to measure
strength. We can place our faith in a seen plan, and keep
control. The way of Jesus seems, in comparison, almost lu-
dicrous. If we yield power to others, we can no longer
trust in ourselves. Trust becomes suddenly a matter of the
size of our God. We must place our faith in an unseen

hand, and divest ourselves of all semblance of control."
(Hybels and Wilkins, *Descending into Greatness*, p. 33.)

The Savior calls us to lose—to lose ourselves in his
work, to forsake notoriety or praise in the accomplishment
of his purposes. He does not ask that we do less than our
best or that we perform less than what is required to do the
job. What he does ask is that we be less concerned with
what others think, less troubled by mortal pecking orders,
less bothered by appearances than we are with reality. In
the work of the ministry, we will be successful in the rescue
of wandering sheep only to the degree that we care more
about the sheep than with how we look, how we come
across, how many sheep we are credited with rescuing, or
how our achievements are publicly acknowledged.

The disciple loses his life when he serves his fellow-
man, when he places others' comfort and convenience before his own. Our Exemplar said: "I am among you as he
that serveth" (Luke 22:27). Service sanctifies both giver
and receiver. Those who involve themselves in the work
of the Master receive the approbation of the Master. As the
unassuming Christ announced: "Break not my commandments for to save your lives; for whosoever will save his
life in this world, shall lose it in the world to come. And
whosoever will lose his life in this world, for my sake,
shall find it in the world to come. Therefore, forsake the
world, and save your souls." (JST Matthew 16:27–29.)

Losing ourselves entails more than being busily engaged in serving others, as essential as that is. It also in-
volves putting off self and putting on Christ. It is the natural man that seeks acclaim, that requires attention, that
elicits compliments. "The natural life in each of us," C. S.
Lewis wrote, "is something self-centered, something that
wants to be petted and admired. . . . And especially it
wants to be left to itself: to keep well away from anything
better or stronger or higher than it, anything that might
make it feel small. It is afraid of the light and air of the

spiritual world, just as people who have been brought up to be dirty are afraid of a bath. And in a sense it is quite right. It knows that if the spiritual life gets hold of it, all its self-centeredness and self-will are going to be killed and it is ready to fight tooth and nail to avoid that." (*Mere Christianity*, p. 154.) A person thus loses himself when he finds Christ, the Captain of his soul. He loses himself when he becomes less concerned with personal whims, more directed toward divine design. She loses herself when she is willing, without let or hindrance, to dedicate herself to the Church of Jesus Christ and to labor with fidelity to assist in the establishment of the kingdom of God on earth.

The Lord calls us to lose—to lose our self-will, our self-promotion, our selfish desires—in favor of a greater and more far-reaching will. He calls us to have an eye single to his glory, to do things his way. Duplicity leads to darkness, while singleness leads to light. "And if your eye be single to my glory, your whole bodies shall be filled with light, and there shall be no darkness in you; and that body which is filled with light comprehendeth all things" (D&C 88:67). The Saints are forevermore sanctified and made holy through yielding their hearts to God (see Helaman 3:35). "When we put God first," President Ezra Taft Benson pointed out, "all other things fall into their proper place or drop out of our lives. Our love of the Lord will govern the claims for our affection, the demands on our time, the interests we pursue, and the order of our priorities." (Conference Report, April 1988, p. 3.)

One of the sad commentaries of this modern age is that so many have lost their way—the way to happiness, the way to peace, the way to genuine fulfillment. It just may be that those who work hardest at trying to find themselves—at least according to this world's standards and methods—will, unfortunately, continue to wander in the morass of existential anguish. Those who turn to the Lord and enter into covenant with him find themselves and

"Woman Taken in Adultery," by James C. Christensen.

"Widow's Mite," by James C. Christensen.

make their way along that strait and narrow path that leads to the abundant life. That life is worth whatever paltry price we have had to pay along the way, and if we attain it, in the end we shall see that there really was no sacrifice at all.

The call to lose is also a call to cooperate. Whereas the worldly seek to put down others through lifting themselves, the Saints are called upon to lift and build and strengthen their brothers and sisters. Whereas too often those driven by the competitive urge seek to abase others through exalting themselves, the Lord directs otherwise. Zion is built upon the principle of cooperation. The people of Zion labor for Zion, "that every man may improve upon his talent, that every man may gain other talents, yea, even an hundred fold . . . every man seeking the interest of his neighbor, and doing all things with an eye single to the glory of God" (D&C 82:18–19). The people of God find no pleasure in defeating others. There is no joy in winning for winning's sake. Rather, there is consummate joy in succoring the weak, lifting up the hands that hang down, and strengthening the feeble knees (see D&C 81:5).

One day things will change. The lowly will be exalted. The unpretentious and the spontaneously (but silent) righteous men and women will be acknowledged from the housetops. Malice and malevolence will melt away as the hoar frost, while benevolence and benificence will become the order of the day. President Howard W. Hunter testified: "In a world too preoccupied with winning through intimidation and seeking to be number one, no large crowd of folk is standing in line to buy books that call for mere meekness. But the meek shall inherit the earth, a pretty impressive corporate takeover—and done *without* intimidation! Sooner or later, and we pray sooner *than* later, everyone will acknowledge that Christ's way is not only the *right* way, but ultimately the *only* way to hope and joy. Every knee shall bow and every tongue will confess that gentleness is better than brutality, that kindness is greater than coercion, that the soft voice turneth away wrath. In the end, and sooner than that whenever possible, we must be more like him." (Conference Report, April 1993, p. 80.)

The Call to Consecrate

Babylon stresses acquisition. Zion calls its citizens to consecration. The Lord doesn't ask for much—he merely wants all of us! The Savior's warning against taking thought for the morrow, what we shall wear or eat (see Matthew 6:25; 3 Nephi 13:25), is actually a warning against undue anxiety about this world's goods and services. The Lord does not want his followers to starve or be undernourished. Nor does he desire that we be unbecoming in appearance or poorly attired. Rather, he calls us to do the right thing for the right reason, to eat to live rather than vice versa, and to clothe our bodies in order that we might be protected from the elements. We need not kneel at the shrines of wooden or stone gods to be idolatrous. We need not offer sacrifice to a lifeless deity to have forsaken the faith of our fathers. Rather, we need only devote the bulk of our time, talents, and means to the establishment or proliferation of a cause other than the gospel cause. False objects of adoration and worship in our day take the form of real estate or portfolios or chrome or furniture or leisure, none of which is innately evil but which as ends in themselves—rather than means—consume and corrupt. Any time things take precedence over persons, particularly the Person of Christ, we are on a downward spiral of personal apostasy. We have wandered off the path of the disciple.

There came to Jesus on one occasion a young man who sought the blessings of eternal life. He inquired as to what was expected of him in order to achieve that glorious end. The Lord specified several of the Ten Commandments, after which the young man responded: "All these have I observed from my youth." Apparently he was a good man, a faithful man, for Mark adds tenderly: "Then Jesus beholding him loved him, and said unto him, One thing thou lackest: go thy way, sell whatsoever thou hast, and give to the poor, and thou shalt have treasure in heaven: and come, take up the cross, and follow me." And then came the moment of truth: "And he [the young man] was sad at that saying, and went away grieved: for he had great possessions." (Mark 10:17–22.)

We ask: Is it necessary to give everything away in order to follow the Christ? In answer, we state simply that apart from the fact that the Church can always use the financial resources of its members to assist in the spreading of the Lord's work throughout the world, the matter of giving up or consecrating one's earthly properties—literally, doing what we do "with sacredness"—is of monumental importance in the formation of a disciple. It strikes at the heart of what it means to come unto Christ. In order to take the yoke of Christ upon us, we must remove the yoke of the world. In order to put on Christ, we must put off the trappings and tinsel of this world.

Jesus said what he meant and meant what he said when he taught that it is easier for a camel to go through the eye of a needle than for a rich man who trusts in his riches to enter into the kingdom of heaven (JST Matthew 19:24; compare JST Mark 10:22–26; JST Luke 18:27). There is no metaphor intended. No softening of this hard saying is justifiable. The issue is one of trust, of reliance, of dependence. The Almighty, who promises us all that he has, asks simply that we be willing to give him all. Nothing else will do. "We are not always called upon to live the whole law of consecration and give all of our time, talents, and means to the building up of the Lord's earthly kingdom," Elder Bruce R. McConkie taught. "Few of us are called upon to sacrifice much of what we possess, and at the moment there is only an occasional martyr in the cause of revealed religion. But what the scriptural account means is that to gain celestial salvation we must be *able* to live these laws to the full if we are called upon to do so. Implicit in this is the reality that we must in fact live them to the extent we are called upon so to do." (Conference Report, April 1975, pp. 74–75.)

It is not that the Lord does not want his people to prosper. In fact, as Dietrich Bonhoeffer observed, "It is not important that I should have no possessions, but if I do I must keep them as though I had them not, in other words I must cultivate a spirit of inward detachment, so that my heart is not in my possessions." (*The Cost of Discipleship*, p. 88.) The anxiety that we mentioned earlier, an anxiety against which the Savior warned his disciples (see Matthew 6:25; 3 Nephi 13:25) is concerned with multiplying my goods, with enhancing my holdings.

The heavens proclaim that "the earth is the Lord's, and the fulness thereof; the world, and they that dwell therein" (Psalm 24:1). In a modern revelation the Lord declared: "Behold, all these properties are mine, or else your faith is vain, and ye are found hypocrites, and the covenants which ye have made unto me are broken; and if the properties are mine, then ye are stewards; otherwise ye are no stewards" (D&C 104:55–56). All things belong to God. He created them and he sustains and upholds them. A vital realization on the part of the man or woman who commits to follow the Redeemer is that he or she owns nothing, that we are stewards over God's properties. The Christian's descent into glory entails an awareness of our nothingness without Deity. King Benjamin thus explained to his people: "I say unto you, my brethren, that if you should render all the thanks and praise which your whole soul has power to possess, to that God who has created you, and has kept and preserved you, . . . I say unto you that if ye should serve him who has created you from the beginning, and is preserving you from day to day, by lending you breath, that ye may live and move and do according to your own will, and even supporting you from one moment to another—I say, if ye should serve him with all your whole souls yet ye would be unprofitable servants." (Mosiah 2:20–21.)

Truly, as Joseph Smith taught in the School of the Prophets, a religion that does not require the sacrifice of all things does not have the power to produce the kind and quality of saving faith in its members that will lead to life and salvation (Lectures on Faith 6:7). Only when the people of the Lord are willing to give their all to the cause of truth—including their own lives, if necessary—do they place themselves in a position to lay hold on the blessings of eternal life. No one wants to die, even to die the death of a martyr. And yet how else could the Lord obtain that unconditional dedication from his people so necessary to the perpetuation of a system of salvation that spans the veil? Only a Church that asks *everything* from its congregants can promise them, in the name of the Lord, everything in eternity.

Conclusion

The call of Christ is a call to humility. "Humble yourselves in the sight of the Lord," James wrote, "and he shall lift you up" (James 4:10). The Christian's descent into glory comes through the surrender of power, through self-abandonment, through servanthood, through sacrifice, and through the ready acknowledgment that without the renovating and transforming graces of the Messiah we are nothing. In this descent, as in all worthy endeavors, Jesus Christ is our Exemplar. "With his life and death as a man, Christ violated every tenet of the world's system. The Highest came to serve the lowest. The Creator and Sustainer of all things came to pour Himself out. The One who possessed everything became nothing. From the world's perspective, the cross became the symbol of foolishness. Yet in God's eyes, Christ became the greatest of the great. . . . And . . . because of Christ's downward mobility, God highly exalted Him, and gave Him a name above every name. That's the twist. Jesus Christ descended into God's greatness." (Hybels and Wilkins, *Descending into Greatness*, p. 19.)

CHAPTER 6

The New Life in Christ

I n 1977 Elder Boyd K. Packer, in a profound message on the role of Christ as the Mediator, declared: "Truth, glorious truth, proclaims there is . . . a Mediator. . . . Through Him mercy can be fully extended to each of us without offending the eternal law of justice. This truth is the very root of Christian doctrine. You may know much about the gospel as it branches out from there, but if you only know the branches and those branches do not touch that root, if they have been cut free from that truth, there will be no life nor substance nor redemption in them." (Conference Report, April 1977, p. 80.) No matter the doctrine, practice, or principle that we teach, if it is not somehow anchored to and grounded in the atonement of the Lord Jesus Christ it will have no life, no staying power. We can ascend to greater spiritual heights only to the degree that we focus on the fundamental reality of Jesus Christ and him crucified.

There is a dimension of the atonement of Christ that perhaps has not received the attention we might have given it, a doctrine taught perhaps most forcefully in the writings of the Apostle Paul. We speak a great deal, and appropriately so, about how Jesus Christ *died for us.* Equally important, though, and often overlooked, is the eternal verity that Christ desires to *live in us.*

Acknowledging Our Fallen Nature

Sometimes, in a day like our own, our young people can grow up in the Church without ever sensing their relationship to the Lord and their need for him. To many, Christ beckons and encourages from offstage: "Go ahead. Do your part. I'll help you when you need it." In reality, he is a Redeemer who comes to make us into new creatures. If we only consider Christ to be "Jesus, my best friend," rather than "Jesus, my Lord and Savior," then we will not know who to call upon in order to be changed and ultimately to be saved.

In short, we do not make much progress in the spiritual realm until we come to acknowledge our need for redemption from a fallen nature. The teaching of the Fall is a very delicate thing. We know that the revelations given to Joseph Smith through the Book of Mormon, his inspired translation of the Bible, and revelations in the Doctrine and Covenants stand as a refreshing breeze of optimism when compared with so much of what was being taught in the Prophet's day about the nature of man. No, we do not believe with Calvin or Luther that man is depraved by nature, that he does not have the capacity to choose good. But there was a fall, and I have come to believe that if the members of the Church do not understand the doctrine of the Fall they never will understand or appreciate the doctrine of atonement. Again, if all we ever teach our young people is how glorious they are, what infinite potential they have, that they are gods in embryo, then when they do sin, and sometimes sin seriously, they really will not know how to handle it.

We know that in the Book of Mormon the doctrine of atonement and the doctrine of the Fall are taught together. They are a package deal. It is difficult to find a place where atonement is taught that the doctrine of the Fall is not taught directly or by implication.

In the New Testament, one chapter in particular has proven problematic over the centuries. The seventh chapter of Romans is often used to illustrate man's inability to even choose what is right. As it reads in the King James Version, we find Paul the poor, stumbling, helpless creature who couldn't do good if he wanted to; in fact, he says in verse 19: "For the good that I would I do not: but the evil which I would not, that I do." That is not the message we need to teach our young people.

The message we need to teach is what is contained in the Joseph Smith Translation (JST) of this chapter. The JST changes a good deal of the chapter, making the emphasis one of "In Christ, I can do all things." Now, the fact is that *we* cannot do all things. It is only in the strength of the Lord that we can do all things. "For all have sinned," Paul explained, "and come short of the glory of God; being justified freely [or "only" as the JST has it] by his grace through the redemption that is in Christ Jesus." (Romans 3:23–24.) President Ezra Taft Benson observed: "Just as a man does not really desire food until he is hungry, so he does not desire the salvation of Christ until he knows why he needs Christ. No one adequately and properly knows why he needs Christ until he understands and accepts the doctrine of the Fall and its effect upon all mankind." (*A Witness and a Warning,* p. 33.)

Going Through the Motions

We are to strive to do good and live the righteous life but to seek at the same time to get beyond simply going through the motions. We have all met people who just go through the motions. Each of us has surely been in that camp at one time or another. We do the right things, but there is no joy in doing so. We are at every meeting; we read the scriptures; we pray regularly; we attend the temple; and we are absolutely burned out. We find little satisfaction in gospel living.

Yes, we do need to do what is right, but I am convinced that enduring to the end is not a matter of simply holding on, white-knuckled-like, gritting our teeth and moving forward. Enduring to the end is intended to be a happy experience. W. Ian Thomas offers this thought:

> There are few things quite so boring as being religious, but there is nothing quite so exciting as being a Christian!
>
> Most folks have never discovered the difference between the one and the other, so that there are those who sincerely try to live a life they do not have, substituting religion for God, Christianity for Christ, and their own noble endeavors for the energy, joy, and power of the Holy Spirit. In the absence of reality, they can only grasp at ritual, stubbornly defending the latter in the absence of the former, lest they be found with neither!
>
> They are lamps without oil, cars without gas, and pens without ink, baffled at their own impotence in the absence of all that alone can make man functional; for *man was so engineered by God that the presence of the Creator within the creature is indispensable to His humanity.* Christ gave Himself for us to give Himself to us! His presence puts God back into the man! He came that we might have life—God's life!
>
> There are those who have a life they never live. *They have come to Christ and thanked Him only for what He did, but do not live in the power of who He is.* Between the Jesus who "was" and the Jesus who "will be" they live in a spiritual

vacuum, trying with no little zeal to live for Christ a life that
only He can live in and through them, perpetually begging
for what in Him they already have! (In Bob George, *Classic
Christianity*, Foreword, emphasis added.)

Going through the motions might be likened to the following situation. Suppose there is a home inhabited by
two kinds of people, those who are absolutely deaf and
those who can hear. One day, a man who can hear goes
into the living room of that home, turns on the stereo, and
begins to listen to some enjoyable music. After a while he
really gets into the music and begins to tap his toe and
snap his fingers. A man who is deaf looks in the doorway
and sees the man sitting on the couch, presumably enjoying what he's doing, tapping his toe and snapping his
fingers. The deaf man asks himself, "I wonder what in the
world he's doing." But because the man on the couch really seems to be enjoying himself, the deaf man goes and
sits down and observes him for a bit longer. Presumably
everyone, even those who cannot hear, has some sense of
rhythm, and so the deaf man begins tapping his toe and
snapping his fingers in time with the other man. The deaf
man thinks to himself, "This is not much fun, but he
surely seems to be enjoying it." So now there are two men
sitting on the couch snapping their fingers, tapping their
toes, and smiling. The plot thickens when a third man
(who can hear) looks in the door and sees the two people
sitting there. What does he conclude? He concludes that
both of the men on the couch are obviously having the
same experience. Nothing could be further from the truth,
for only one of them hears the music. (Example cited in
George, *Classic Christianity*, pp. 152–53.)

Life in Christ is hearing the music. Yes, we must strive
to do what is right. Yes, we should do our home and vis-
iting teaching in the sense that we visit our families and
care for them, even when we are not eager to do so. We
cannot just leave the work of the kingdom to others because

we have not been changed and reborn, but that doesn't mean we have to always remain that way. We may change; we can change; we should change; and it is the Lord who can and will change us.

Being Filled

Coming unto Christ entails more than being cleansed, as important as that is. It entails being *filled*. We speak often of the importance of being cleansed or sanctified. It is to have the Holy Spirit, who is not only a revelator but a sanctifier, remove filth and dross from our souls as though by fire. We refer to this as a baptism by fire. To be cleansed is essential, but to stop there is to stop short of great blessings. It would be like finding my wife in the kitchen boiling twenty jars in a large container on the stove. I say to her, "Shauna, what are you doing?"

"Sterilizing jars," she answers.

I ask, "Why are you sterilizing the jars?"

"To get them clean."

"What are you going to do with the clean jars?"

"Put them on the cupboard."

"What are you going to do with them there?"

"I'm going to put them there so everyone can see just how clean they are."

"What purpose will they serve?"

"People will know we have clean jars." (Example cited in George, *Classic Christianity*, p. 62.)

Now, the fact of the matter is this—the jars will serve precious little function just because they are clean. They need to be filled. It is the same with us. It isn't enough to have the Lord clean us out through the Holy Spirit. He must fill us. That word *fill* is used repeatedly in scripture, especially the Book of Mormon.

Paul presents the idea of (in a sense) nailing ourselves to the cross of Christ—nailing our old selves, the old man of sin. He writes: "I am crucified with Christ: *nevertheless I live; yet not I, but Christ liveth in me*: and the life which I now live in the flesh I live by the faith of the Son of God, who loved me, and gave himself for me" (Galatians 2:20, emphasis added). That is a new life in Christ. To the Ephesian Saints Paul wrote: "For by grace are ye saved through faith; and that not of yourselves: it is the gift of God: not of works, lest any man should boast. For *we are his workmanship, created in Christ Jesus unto good works*, which God hath before ordained that we should walk in them." (Ephesians 2:8–10, emphasis added.) When we have been filled, the Spirit is with us, and Christ comes to dwell in us through that Spirit as he desires to do. Then our works begin to be motivated by that Holy Spirit and they are no longer our works; they are his works.

The risen Lord said to the Nephites that there were certain things required before his church would be his Church: it had to have his name, and it must be built upon his gospel. If these two conditions were met, then the Father would show forth his own works in it. (See 3 Nephi 27:5–10.) How? Through the body of Christ, the members of the Church. The Holy Spirit motivates them to greater righteousness. It is not expected that we "go through the motions" all our lives. There can come a time when my motives, desires, and yearnings have been changed, and I begin to do the works in the way God would do them, because he has now begun to live in me through his Spirit.

On another occasion Paul wrote: "Wherefore, my beloved, as ye have always obeyed, not as in my presence only, but now much more in my absence, work out your own salvation with fear and trembling." If we stop our reading there, we wonder about the phrase "work out your own salvation." How? There's not a person living on this earth that can work out his or her own salvation, at least not without divine assistance. There aren't enough home teaching visits, there aren't enough cakes and pies to be delivered to the neighbors, there aren't enough prayers to be uttered, for a person to work out his own salvation. But Paul doesn't stop there. He added: "For it is God which worketh in you both to will and to do of his good pleasure." (Philippians 2:12–13.) The works are the Lord's works through us, and thus we are doing not our works but his works.

One more scripture further illustrates this point— Ephesians 5:17–18: "Wherefore be ye not unwise, but understanding what the will of the Lord is. And be not drunk with wine, wherein is excess; but be filled with the Spirit." Another way Paul could have said that is, "Don't be drunk with wine, but be drunk with the Spirit." To be drunk implies more than having imbibed something. It means more than to fill up. To be drunk with something is to be under the control of that substance, to actually surrender one's body. If I am drunk with liquor, I have essentially surrendered myself to that substance. I've surrendered my mind and my spirit to its influence. Coming to Christ, then, entails more than being cleansed. It entails being filled, coming under his influence.

A Change of Nature

Through the atonement of Christ we do more than enjoy a change of behavior; we come to change our *nature*. "Therefore, if any man be in Christ, he is a new creature: old things are passed away; behold, all things are become new" (2 Corinthians 5:17). Isn't that what King Benjamin was being taught by the angel—that the natural man is an enemy to God and will stay that way unless and until he yields himself to the enticings of the Holy Spirit? (See Mosiah 3:19.) John Stott has explained: "We may be quite sure that Christ-centeredness and Christ-likeness will never be attained by our own unaided efforts. How can self drive out self? As well expect Satan to drive out Satan! For we are not interested in skin-deep holiness, in a merely external resemblance to Jesus Christ. . . . What we long for is a deep inward change of character, resulting from a change of nature and leading to a radical change of conduct. In a word we want to be *like Christ,* and that thoroughly, profoundly, entirely. Nothing less than this will do." (*Life in Christ,* p. 109.)

Elder Glenn Pace put it in this way: "We should all be striving for a disposition to do no evil, but to do good continually. This isn't a resolve or a discipline; it is a disposition. We do things because we want to, not just because we know we should. . . . Sometimes we overlook the fact that a spiritual transformation or metamorphosis must take place within us. It comes about through grace and by the Spirit of God, although it does not come about until we have truly repented and proven ourselves worthy. We can be guilty of being so careful to live the letter of the law that we don't develop our inner spiritual nature and fine-tune our spiritual communication to the point that we may receive sanctification and purification. My conclusion is that we will not be saved by works if those works are not born of a disposition to do good, as opposed to an obligation to do good." (*Spiritual Plateaus,* pp. 62–63.) This, of course, is what President Ezra Taft Benson meant when he taught that although the world deals in externals, the Lord works from the inside out (see Conference Report, October 1985, p. 5).

The Great Exchange

The Lord Jesus Christ came to earth not only to change us, but to *exchange* with us. He creates in us a new identity. Note Paul's words in Philippians 3:8–9: "Yea doubtless, and I count all things but loss for the excellency of the knowledge of Christ Jesus my Lord: for whom I have suffered the loss of all things, and do count them but dung, that I may win Christ. And *be found in him, not having mine own righteousness, which is of the law, but that which is through the faith of Christ, the righteousness which is of God by faith.*" (Emphasis added.) Paul wrote also that Christ has reconciled us to the Father and has delivered to his followers the "ministry of reconciliation." That is, our Mediator has reconciled us to the Father through the Atonement and asked us to extend those glad tidings to others. "To wit, that God was in Christ, reconciling the world unto himself, not imputing their trespasses unto them; and hath committed unto us the word of reconciliation [the gospel]. Now then we are ambassadors for Christ, as though God did beseech you by us [that is, He is working through his legal administrators to save souls]: we pray you in Christ's stead, be ye reconciled to God. For he [God the Father] hath made him [Christ the Son] to be sin for us, who knew no sin; that we might be made the righteousness of God in him." (2 Corinthians 5:17–21.)

One of the eternal ironies of the Atonement is that in Gethsemane and on Golgotha our Lord and Savior, "he who had never known sin" and never taken a backward step or a spiritual detour, became the great "sinner." The Lord not only changes our nature, but he offers to exchange with us. He takes the sin. He imputes to us his righteousness. That is the only way we can become righteous in eternity. That is the only way people become perfect. People do not become perfect just by striving and striving to do the right things. They become *perfect in Christ*. He imputes to them his perfection. These are they who are made perfect through the atonement of Christ (see D&C 76:69). And so, he comes to exchange us, and in that sense to provide a new identity, such that we do not have to identify with that old identity anymore.

One writer described the transformation in this way:

> Being made into a new creation is like a caterpillar becoming a butterfly. Originally an earthbound crawling creature, a caterpillar weaves a cocoon and is totally immersed

in it. Then a marvelous process takes place called metamorphosis. Finally a totally new creature—a butterfly—emerges. Once ground-bound, the butterfly can now soar above the earth. It now can view life from the sky downward. In the same way, as a new creature in Christ you must begin to see yourself as God sees you.

If you were to see a butterfly, it would never occur to you to say, "Hey, everybody! Come look at this good-looking, converted worm!" Why not? After all, it was a worm. And it was "converted." No, now it is a new creature, and you don't think of it in terms of what it was. You see it as it is now—a butterfly. (Bob George, *Classic Christianity*, p. 78.)

The Fruit of the Spirit

One of the marks of our discipleship, one of the significant evidences of our growth into this new life in Christ, is the degree to which we have begun to enjoy the fruit of the Spirit. In three different books of scripture the Lord discusses the *gifts* of the Spirit—such things as discernment, tongues, interpretation of tongues, gifts of administration, prophecy, healing, and so forth. It is interesting that in 1 Corinthians 12 Paul suggests that the gifts of the Spirit are intended to enhance, build up, and make perfect the body of Christ, meaning the Church. It is for the good of the Church and the kingdom. Certainly related, but not necessarily to be confused with the gifts of the Spirit, however, are the fruit of the Spirit. In Galatians chapter five Paul begins by contrasting the works of the flesh with the fruit of the spirit: "Now the works of the flesh are manifest, which are these; Adultery, fornication, uncleanness, lasciviousness, idolatry, witchcraft, hatred, variance, emulations, wrath, strife, seditions, heresies, envyings, murders, drunkenness, revellings, and such like: of the which I tell you before, as I have also told you in time past, that they which do such things shall not inherit the kingdom of God" (Galatians 5:19–21).

We recall that for each of us there are two births. There is a natural birth and there is a spiritual birth. The natural birth comes with mortality, and the natural birth creates the natural man. The spiritual birth comes later. The natural birth has its own set of fruits or works. We have just noted Paul's mention of several of them. The spiritual man or woman brings forth his or her own fruits. "But the fruit of the Spirit is love, joy, peace, longsuffering, gentleness, goodness, faith, meekness, temperance: against such there is no law. And they that are Christ's have crucified the flesh with the affections and lusts. If we live in the Spirit, let us also walk in the Spirit." (Galatians 5:22–25.)

The gifts that we know as the gifts of the Spirit, things that probably began to develop before we came here—aptitudes, capacities, talents, and so forth—usually come quite naturally for us. For many of us the gift of speaking or the gift of teaching comes naturally, and these are spiritual gifts. For others such gifts as discernment or wisdom are an integral part of their lives. But there are people who are wonderful speakers but horrible Christians. We can have one and not have the other. There are people who do remarkable things in the classroom and do sad things outside the classroom. (Talk to their families, secretaries, staff, or co-workers.) The gifts of the Spirit are one thing, the fruit of the Spirit another. Patience, mercy, meekness, gentleness, longsuffering, and, of course, charity or the pure love of Christ—these are the kinds of things that begin to characterize men and women who have begun to live in Christ. Such persons are simply more Christ-like. Elder Marion D. Hanks frequently asked a haunting question, one that strikes at the core of this matter. He inquired: "If you were arrested and were to be tried for being a Christian, would there be enough evidence to convict you?"

The interesting thing about the fruit of the Spirit is that such attitudes and such actions do not seem to be situational. In other words, a person is not just very fruitful in the Spirit while the sun shines, pleasant and kindly only when circumstances are positive. Rather, those who enjoy the fruit of the Spirit feel love for those who do not love in return, joy in the midst of painful circumstances, peace when something counted upon doesn't come through, patience when things are not going fast enough, kindness towards those who treat others unkindly, goodness towards those who have been intentionally insensitive, faithfulness when friends have proven unfaithful, gentleness towards those who have acted roughly, self-control in the midst of intense temptation. (See Charles Stanley, *The Wonderful Spirit-Filled Life*, p. 108.)

Our challenge is to learn to *abide in Christ*. Jesus taught that he is the vine and we are the branches (see John 15:1–8). We tend to get ourselves in trouble sometimes when we see ourselves as the producers of fruit. We are at best the *bearers* of fruit. In that sense, may I suggest that we should do all we can do by way of living a good life, but that, given what we have considered so far, especially in the writings of Paul, it is not *difficult* to live the Christian life. It is *impossible!* At least, it is impossible by ourselves. It is only as the Lord assists us in that endeavor that we are able to bring to pass great things. A Protestant minister notes: "If you do not learn to abide in Christ, you will never have a marriage characterized by love, joy, and peace. You will never have the self-control necessary to consistently overcome temptation. And you will always be an emotional hostage of your circumstances. Why? Because apart from abiding in Christ, you can do nothing.

"Jesus makes a clear delineation between the vine and the branch. The two are not the same. *He* is the vine; *we* are the branches. The two are joined but not one. The common denominator in nature is the sap. The sap is the life of the vine and its branches. Cut off the flow of sap to the branch, and it slowly withers and dies. As the branch draws its life from the vine, so we draw life from Christ. *To abide in Christ is to draw upon His life.*" (Stanley, *The Wonderful Spirit-Filled Life*, p. 64.)

Conclusion

We do not come to cultivate the fruit of the Spirit by always talking about fruit. We cultivate, gain, and enjoy the fruit of the Spirit by seeking the Spirit. Likewise, we do not become new creatures in Christ through lengthy discussions on the new birth, but by seeking a remission of sins and by pleading to be filled with that sacred Spirit that fills as well as sanctifies. I have come to know that there is a power beyond anything we could ever work ourselves into. We strive to do the works of righteousness, and that is how we keep our part of the covenant, but we plead all along that Christ re-create us in his image. There is a life in Christ, a more abundant life, a restful and peaceful life. C. S. Lewis has observed that this change in perspective, this growth into a new life in Christ, "is precisely what Christianity is about. This world is a great sculptor's shop. We are the statues and there is a rumour going round the shop that some of us are some day going to come to life." (*Mere Christianity*, p. 140.)

some of the despondency and guilt associated with falling short of my goals, of trying to do it all, of striving to make myself perfect. I have been associated with many wonderful, caring people who struggle occasionally with feelings of inadequacy, who hope against hope that one day— in some distant age in the future—in spite of their frailty in this sphere they might qualify to go and feel comfortable where Gods and angels are. Since it is true that the gospel of Jesus Christ is intended to liberate us, to ease and lighten our burdens, to bring that comfort and rest found in no other way, why is it that some of us struggle at times? Why is it that once in a while we find ourselves simply going through the motions, doing our duty in the Church but finding little fulfillment and enjoyment in it?

I suspect that many Latter-day Saints will agree to the same faulty orientation I found in myself. My greatest frustrations seem to have come as a result of my efforts to "handle it" myself, or, in other words, my failure to trust in and rely on the Lord. Maybe it's our culture that contributes to our dilemma; maybe it's the constant chants of "You can do anything you put your mind to," or "You have unlimited possibilities and potential," that tend to focus our attention away from the powers of the divine toward our abilities, our merits, and our contributions. I have come to know that the answer to our problems is not to be found alone in humanity, no matter how impressive our accomplishments. The solution to the soul's yearning for solace is not to be located in the programs of society per se. In a way, we almost need to work at cross purposes to social trends, to attune our ears to a quiet voice that beckons to us amidst the loud babble of competing voices. That quiet voice pleads with us simply to come unto Christ. The answer to individual hurt and personal pain is not to be found solely in congressional decisions or developments in personnel management, not in louder cries of victimization, but in and through Jesus Christ. The most pertinent crusade in which the Christian is involved is the quest for personal peace and the campaign for purity of heart, all of which comes from Christ through the ordinances of the priesthood and by the power of the Holy Ghost. The scriptures teach plainly and persuasively that coming unto Christ entails a moment of decision. It is that poignant point in our progression wherein we realize that man-made solutions are in reality "broken cisterns that can hold no water" (Jeremiah 2:13) and that only through yoking ourselves to the Master may we rid ourselves of the burdens of Babylon.

Who's in Control?

Few things in this life are exactly as they seem to be. We live in a time, for example, when everyone is told of the importance of being in control. We must be in charge. We must have access to and management over all the variables. We operate by plans and formulae and procedures. Lists and tables and charts abound. One of the harsh realities facing someone acclimated to this fallen world is that spiritual things are not programmable. We cannot require or demand or shape spiritual experience. The Spirit is in control, not us. The Lord through his Spirit works his marvelous wonders in his own time, in his own way, and according to his own will and purposes. To enter the realm of divine experience, therefore, is to enter a realm where we are not in complete control. We can seek to be worthy, strive to be in a position to be blessed, plead and pray for divine intervention; but we do not force the hand of the Almighty.

Though such matters as self-reliance and self-confidence may prove to be valuable in some of our dealings in this life, the reciprocal principles of submission, surrender, and having an eye single to the glory of God are essential if we are to acquire that enabling power described in scripture as the saving grace of Jesus Christ. It is as if the Lord inquires of us: "Do you want to be a possessor of all things such that all things are subject unto you?" We of course respond in the affirmative. He then says: "Good. Then submit to me. Yield your heart unto me." The Lord asks further: "Do you want to have victory over all things?" We nod. He follows up: "Then surrender to me. Unconditionally." Odd, isn't it? We incorporate the powers of divinity only through acknowledging our own inabilities, accepting our limitations, and realizing our weakness. We open ourselves to infinite strength only through accepting our finite condition. We in time gain control through being willing to relinquish control.

Too much of my own frustration over the years has come as a result of my refusal to let go and thus let God. Something—I suppose it is the natural man, the prideful self that automatically asserts its own agenda—drives me to want to do it myself. Oh, I believe in God, to be sure, that he loves me, that he sent his Son to earth to help me. All too often, however, my actions have betrayed my limited orientation, my vision of Christ as a type of spiritual advisor, a sort of celestial cheerleader who stands on the sidelines and whispers encouragement, but not the Lord God Omnipotent who came to earth to make men and women into new creatures through empowering them to do what they could never do for themselves. Too many of my efforts, and unfortunately too many of my prayers, have been bent on succeeding—according to my own predetermined plan. Instead of opening myself to divine direction and incorporating the powers of heaven, I wanted to be able to look back on life and sing with gusto, "I did it my way!" Too little time was spent in sacred submission; on too few occasions did I say the words (and mean it!), "Thy will be done, O Lord, and not mine." Instead of praying to know my limits, to know when my offering was acceptable, I prayed for more drive and more willpower. I have since come to believe that "fallen man is not simply an imperfect creature who needs improvement: he is a rebel who must lay down his arms" (C. S. Lewis, *Mere Christianity*, p. 59). The saving and ironic truth is: As we submit, we come to know his will. As we surrender, we come to gain his power. As we yield our hearts to God, our affections and our feelings are sanctified by his grace. As President Ezra Taft Benson has taught, once we turn our lives over to the Lord we discover that he can do far more with us than we could ever do with ourselves (see *The Teachings of Ezra Taft Benson*, p. 361).

In Whom Do I Trust?

There is a passage in the Book of Mormon that can be rather frightening. Jacob explained: "And [Christ] commandeth all men that they must repent, and be baptized in his name, having perfect faith in the Holy One of Israel, or they cannot be saved in the kingdom of God" (2 Nephi 9:23). Perfect faith. *Perfect* faith! Who do you know that has perfect faith, at least as we tend to gauge perfection? I suggest that Jacob is here driving at a point that we are prone to miss—that those who have perfect faith in the Holy One of Israel are those who have learned to trust in him completely, to trust in his purposes as well as his timetable. To come out of the world is to realize that we cannot place our trust in the world. "To come out of the world," President Stephen L Richards observed, "one must forsake the philosophy of the world, and to come into Zion one must adopt the philosophy of Zion. In my own thinking I have reduced the process to a very simple formula: Forsake the philosophy of self-sufficiency, which is the philosophy of the world, and adopt the philosophy of faith, which is the philosophy of Christ. Substitute faith for self-assurance." (*Where Is Wisdom?*, p. 419.)

If I trust completely (or perfectly) in Christ, then how much do I trust in myself? Answer: None. My works are necessary. My reception of the ordinances, the performance

of my duties in the Church, acts of service and kindness—
these are a part of my Christian covenantal obligation.
They are the things I can do, at least the things I can do my
best at. But let us come face to face with the reality that
there are not enough loaves of bread, enough home or vis-
iting teaching appointments, or enough encouraging notes
to assure my exaltation. My good works are necessary, but
they are not sufficient. I cannot work myself into celestial
glory, and I cannot guarantee myself a place among the
sanctified through my own unaided efforts. Therefore,
even though my own merits are essential to salvation, it is
not by my own merits that I will ever make it. Rather, it is
by and through the merits of Christ. This transcendent
truth should create not feelings of futility but feelings of
humility.

Lehi addressed his son Jacob with these words:
"Wherefore, I know that thou art redeemed. . . ." Why was
he redeemed? Because he was such an obedient son?
Because he had followed the direction of his older
brother? Because he was sensitive and submissive and
faithful? We know that he was all of that. But note Lehi's
words: "Wherefore, I know that thou art redeemed, because of the righteousness of thy Redeemer" (2 Nephi 2:3).
Jacob was bound for glory because of the goodness of
Jesus! But didn't Jacob's goodness matter? Of course it
did; Jacob's carefulness to live according to the commandments evidenced his commitment to the Lord and his desire to keep his part of the covenant. But as noble a son as
Jacob was, he could never save himself. As a modern revelation attests, Christ pleads our cause before the Father on
the basis of *his* suffering and death and perfection (see
D&C 45:3–5). Imperfect people can only be redeemed by a
perfect Being.

Nephi encouraged his readers to rely "wholly upon the
merits of him who is mighty to save" (2 Nephi 31:19).
Aaron explained that "since man had fallen he could not
merit anything of himself; but the sufferings and death of

Christ atone for their sins, through faith and repentance" (Alma 22:14). Moroni added that the Saints of God rely "alone upon the merits of Christ, who [is] the author and the finisher of [our] faith" (Moroni 6:4). We are indeed saved by merit, but by the merits of our Redeemer. The debate has raged for far too long as to whether we are saved by grace or by works, a squabble into which too many of the Latter-day Saints have been drawn. It is a silly argument, an unnecessary struggle, one that has generated much more heat than light. It is, in fact, the wrong question. The real questions—the ones that get to the heart of the matter—are: In whom do I trust? On whom do I rely? Truly, as someone has suggested, the word *grace* makes an acronym for a glorious concept—"*G*od's *R*iches *A*t *C*hrist's *E*xpense" (John F. MacArthur, Jr., *Faith Works: The Gospel According to the Apostles*, p. 57).

My confidence in God is essential. My confidence in myself is incidental, inextricably tied to my trust in God. As Bruce Hafen has observed: "When we place our confidence in God rather than in ourselves, our need for self-esteem takes care of itself—not because of our manipulation of successful experiences but because our fundamental attitude allows us access to the only trustworthy source for knowing that the course of life we pursue is known to and accepted by God. It is not just the mistake-free, no-fault life that pleases God. He has deliberately placed us in a sphere where the most sharply focused purpose is to learn from our experience and to grow in both our desires and our understanding to be like him. Obviously that includes the greatest effort and integrity we can muster as we seek to do his will. But the heart of it all is not *self*-confidence. It is confidence in *him*, and in his power to make us into creatures far beyond the reach of what our goal-setting and goal-achieving can ultimately accomplish in the process of becoming as he is." (*The Broken Heart*, p. 120.)

In summary, then, there is a life, a life in Christ, a new life in Christ that we cannot know or experience unless we yield to and appropriate his transforming powers and stop trying to do everything ourselves. In the spiritual realm, there is nothing weak about trusting, nothing passive about reliance. In one sense, as C. S. Lewis observed, "the road back to God is a road of moral effort, of trying harder and harder. But in another sense it is not trying that is ever going to bring us home. All this trying leads up to the vital moment at which you turn to God and say, 'You must do this. I can't.'" Such submission, Lewis adds, represents a significant change, "the change from being confident about our own efforts to the state in which we despair of doing anything for ourselves and leave it to God.

"I know the words 'leave it to God' can be misunderstood," Lewis continues. "The sense in which a Christian leaves it to God is that he puts all his trust in Christ: trusts that Christ will somehow share with him the perfect human obedience which he carried out from His birth to His crucifixion: that Christ will make the man [or woman] more like Himself and, in a sense, make good his [or her] deficiencies." (*Mere Christianity*, p. 128.)

In a word, I am incomplete or partial, while Christ is whole or complete. As I come unto Christ by covenant, we (Christ and I) are complete. I am unfinished, while Christ is finished. Through "relying alone" upon the merits of the author and finisher of my faith (Moroni 6:4; compare Hebrews 12:2), I become finished or fully formed. I am oh, so imperfect, while Christ is perfect. Together we are perfect. Truly, as the Apostle Paul taught, we "are complete in him, [who] is the head of all principality and power" (Colossians 2:9–10). Those who come unto Christ become perfect *in him* (Moroni 10:32). Those who inherit the celestial kingdom are just men and just women who have been "made perfect through Jesus the mediator of the new covenant, who wrought out this perfect atonement through the shedding of his own blood" (D&C 76:69).

Conclusion

These principles have been in the scriptures all along. They have been a part of Mormonism since the beginning and have been an integral part of the lives of those Latter-day Saints whose trust in the Lord was greater than their trust in other things. Living by grace is a way of life, an understanding, a perspective that comes to *us* as we come unto *him* who is the embodiment of peace and rest. Perhaps it is the complexity of life in a modern world that has driven many of us to our knees more frequently and caused us to search the scriptures with an earnestness born of pressing need. And perhaps it is our rediscovery of the Book of Mormon, Another Testament of Jesus Christ, that has led some of us to recognize through study what we have begun to know by faith. We sense more than ever the need to do our duty, to attend to our family and Church responsibilities, all as a part of keeping our covenant with Christ. That is, we come to know the value and necessity of good works. Those works come to be motivated by his Spirit and evidence our covenant. But we also seek for that balance, that critical and elusive balance in life, that allows us to do our best without browbeating ourselves because of all we cannot do at the moment.

I believe the Lord wants us to succeed and that he has every intention of bringing back as many of his children as is possible. Discouragement and despondency are not of the Lord. They are of Lucifer. The arch-deceiver would have us lose our balance, lose track of what matters most in life, and focus too much on the less significant. He would have us labor to exhaustion in secondary causes. We cannot do everything we are asked to do, at least not in a few weeks or months. There is great virtue in praying that the Lord will reveal to us our limits, let us know when doubling or tripling our efforts will in reality be spiritually counterproductive.

Because we are human—because we are weak and mortal and tired—we will probably never reach the point in this life when we have done "all we can do." Too many of us misread 2 Nephi 25:23 and conclude that the Lord can assist us only *after*, meaning following the time that, we have done "all we can do." That is incorrect; he can and does help us all along the way. I think Nephi is trying to emphasize that no matter how much we do, it simply will not be enough to guarantee salvation without Christ's intervention. Restating Nephi, "Above and beyond all we can do, it is by the grace of Christ that we are saved." And what is true of our ultimate salvation is true of our daily walk and talk, of our personality and our passions. Above and beyond all efforts at self-control, behavior modification, or reducing our sins to manageable categories, "everything which really needs to be done in our souls can be done only by God" (C. S. Lewis, *Mere Christianity*, p. 165).

To push ourselves beyond what is appropriate is, in a strange sort of way, a statement that we fear we must do the job ourselves if we expect it to get done. I know we must do our duty in the Church and that the works of righteousness are necessary. What seems so very unnecessary is the type of pharisaical extremism and the subsequent negative feelings that too often characterize the efforts of some members of the Church. I have a conviction that God is unquestionably aware of us. He loves you and he loves me. This I know. He certainly wants us to improve, but he definitely does not want us to spend our days languishing in guilt. I reaffirm that the gospel of Jesus Christ is intended to liberate us, to lift and lighten our burdens. If despite our diligent efforts it is not doing that in our personal lives, then perhaps our approach and understanding, our orientation—not necessarily the quantity of work to be done—need some adjustment.

Too often Latter-day Saints are prone to view the grace of God as that increment of goodness, that extra spiritual boost, that is provided as a free gift by the Almighty on

Judgment Day to make it possible for us to go into the celestial kingdom. It is certainly true that we will need a full measure of divine assistance to become celestial material. But the grace of God, through Jesus Christ our Lord, is available to us every hour and every day of our lives. "True grace," as one writer has suggested, "is more than just a giant freebie, opening the door to heaven in the sweet by and by, but leaving us to wallow in sin in the bitter here and now. Grace is God presently at work in our lives" (MacArthur, *Faith Works*, p. 32).

I know of the power that is in Christ, power not only to create the worlds and divide the seas but also to still the storms of the human heart, to right life's wrongs, to ease and eventually even remove the pain of scarred and beaten souls. There is no bitterness, no anger, no fear, no jealousy, no feelings of inadequacy that cannot be healed by the Great Physician. He is the Balm of Gilead. He is the One sent by the Father to "bind up the brokenhearted, to proclaim liberty to the captives, and the opening of the prison to them that are bound" (Isaiah 61:1).

"*Learn* of me," Jesus said in the meridian of time, "for I am meek and lowly in heart: and ye shall find rest unto your souls" (Matthew 11:29, emphasis added). "*Learn* of me," that same Lord beckoned in a modern revelation, "and listen to my words; walk in the meekness of my Spirit, and you shall have peace in me" (D&C 19:23, emphasis added). True followers of Christ learn to trust in him more, in the arm of flesh less. They learn to rely on him more, on man-made solutions less. They learn to surrender their burdens to him more. They learn to work to their limits and then be willing to seek that grace or enabling power that will make up the difference, that sacred power that makes all the difference! Theirs is a quiet confidence in the Lord's promise that he will never forsake his own: "The soul that on Jesus hath leaned for repose/I will not, I cannot, desert to his foes;/That soul, though all hell should endeavor to shake,/I'll never, no never, no never

"Christ Laments Over Jerusalem," by Gary E. Smith.

"Christ in Gethsemane," by James C. Christensen.

Christt the Center

We began this book with a testimony that Mormons are indeed Christian, that Jesus of Nazareth is the fundamental reality of our faith, and that a firm base for life and light and hope and happiness is to be found in him, his gospel, and the teachings and ordinances of his Restored Church or they are to be found not at all. Let us now, by way of conclusion, once again turn our attention to him who is the Holy One and express how it is we relate to this Jesus who is called Christ. What, then, do the scriptures—ancient and modern—teach in regard to men's and women's relationship to the Lord of Life?

On Christ

Every person builds a house of faith. We do so either knowingly or unknowingly. And every builder soon learns that a good building with a bad foundation is worse than useless; it is dangerous. As one Christian writer has observed: "If the stability of buildings depends largely on their foundations, so does the stability of human lives. The search for personal security is a primal instinct, but many fail to find it today. Old familiar landmarks are being obliterated. Moral absolutes which were once thought to be eternal are being abandoned." (John Stott, *Life in Christ*, p. 22.) Thus our house of faith can be no more secure than the foundation upon which it is built. Foolish men build upon the shifting sands of ethics and the marshlands of human philosophies and doctrines. The wise build upon the rock of revelation, heeding carefully the living oracles, lest they be "brought under condemnation . . . and stumble and fall when the storms descend, . . . and beat upon their house" (D&C 90:5). All that we do as members of The Church of Jesus Christ of Latter-day Saints must be built upon a foundation of faith and testimony and conversion. When external supports fail us, then our hearts must be riveted upon the things of the Spirit, those internal realities that provide the meaning, the perspective, and the sustenance for all else that matters in life.

As a type of climax to a commission delivered to his sons, Helaman said: "And now, my sons, remember, remember that it is upon the rock of our Redeemer, who is Christ, the Son of God, that ye must build your foundation; that when the devil shall send forth his mighty winds, yea, his shafts in the whirlwind, yea, when all his hail and his mighty storm shall beat upon you, it shall have no power over you to drag you down to the gulf of misery and endless wo, because of the rock upon which ye are built, which is a sure foundation, a foundation whereon if men build they cannot fall" (Helaman 5:12). Surely the supreme challenge of this life for those of us who aspire to Christian discipleship is to build our lives on Christ, to erect our house of faith, a divine domicile in which he and his Spirit would be pleased to dwell. There is safety from Satan and his minions only in Christ. There is security only in his word and through his infinite and eternal power.

How, then, do we build on Christ? In a day when the winds are blowing and the waves are beating upon our ship, how do we navigate our course safely into the peaceful harbor? What must we do to have our Savior pilot us through life's tempestuous seas? Amidst the babble of voices—discordant but enticing voices that threaten to lead us into forbidden paths or that beckon us to labor in secondary causes—how do the Saints of the Most High know the Way, live the Truth, and gain that Life that is abundant? The revelations and the prophets offer us some simple yet far-reaching suggestions:

1. *Treasure up his word.* The scriptures are the words of Christ. They contain the warnings and doctrinal teachings of those who were moved upon by the Holy Ghost and who thus spoke with the tongue of angels (see 2 Nephi 31:13; 32:1–3; 33:10). To read and ponder them is to hear the voice of the Master (D&C 18:34–36). Those who cherish and are grounded in the scriptures are more equipped to sift and sort through the sordid, more prepared to distinguish the divine from the diabolical, the sacred from the secular.

2. *Teach his doctrine.* There is a supernal power that accompanies the plain and direct teaching of doctrine. The views and philosophies of men—no matter how pleasingly they are stated or how lofty and timely they may seem—simply cannot engage the soul in the same way the doctrines of the gospel can. If we teach doctrine, particularly the doctrine of Christ, and if we do so with the power and persuasion of the Holy Ghost, our listeners will be turned to Christ.

3. *Sustain his servants.* As we discussed earlier, to receive the Lord's servants is to accept their word as the word of Deity, to accept their authority as God's authority. Certainly no one could accept the Father while rejecting the Son, and likewise no one can accept the Son while rejecting the teachings and direction of those the Savior has commissioned to act in his name. No person comes to the

Master who does not acknowledge the mantle worn by his anointed.

4. *Trust in and rely on the Lord.* It is through trusting in the promises and purposes of the Lord—his timetable as well as his tutoring—that we come to have perfect faith in the Holy One of Israel (see 2 Nephi 9:23). As we work to our limits and then seek that divine grace or enabling power spoken of in the scriptures, the Master supplements and sanctifies our poor offering and we eventually become perfect in Christ.

In short, we must build our lives *on Christ.* He must become our foundation. As a hymn from an earlier century has it:

> My hope is built on nothing less
> than Jesus' blood and righteousness;
> no merit of my own I claim,
> but wholly trust in Jesus' name.
> > On Christ, the solid rock, I stand—
> > all other ground is sinking sand.
>
> When weary in this earthly race,
> I rest on his unchanging grace;
> in every wild and stormy gale
> my anchor holds and will not fail.
>
> His vow, his covenant and blood
> are my defence against the flood;
> when earthly hopes are swept away
> he will uphold me on that day.
>
> When the last trumpet's voice shall sound,
> O may I then in him be found!
> clothed in his righteousness alone,
> faultless to stand before his throne.
> > On Christ, the solid rock, I stand—
> > all other ground is sinking sand.
>
> (Edward Mote, as cited in John Stott, *Life in Christ,* p. 29.)

Through Christ

"I am the way, the truth, and the life," Jesus said in the meridian of time; "no man cometh unto the Father, but by me" (John 14:6). Because of the Fall, all men and women are estranged from the things of righteousness, and more particularly, alienated from the family of God. The scriptures declare that all persons—every man, woman, and child that belong to the family of Adam—are lost and fallen, and will remain subject to spiritual death unless and until they are extricated, through the intervention of divine powers, from this benighted condition. One does not go from a lost to a found condition through group therapy or values clarification. One does not go from misery and spiritual listlessness to sacred security merely through setting goals and achieving them. In short, one is not transformed from darkness to light, from death to life, from an inert to a quickened condition, except through the mediation of the Master. Jesus came to earth to reconcile us to the Father.

The gulf that exists between God and man may have come initially through the fall of Adam (the fall of *man*), but it is maintained and broadened through individual inertia and individual sin (the fall of *me*). As has been wisely observed: "Apart from Jesus Christ, then, the chasm between God and us is impassable. It is our human finitude on the one hand, and our self-centered rebellion on the other. By ourselves we can neither know God nor reach him. The pathetic little bridges we build from our side all fall into the abyss. Only one bridge spans the otherwise unbridgeable gulf. It has been thrown across from the other side. It is Jesus Christ, God's eternal Son." (John Stott, *Life in Christ*, p. 11.) That chasm is spanned through two means—the *revelation* of Jesus Christ, which speaks to our ignorance, and the *redemption* of Jesus Christ, which speaks to our sinfulness. God's willingness that we be reconciled and his desire that we return to his presence is evidenced in his infinite gift: "For God so loved the world, that he gave his only begotten Son, that whosoever believeth in him should not perish, but have everlasting life" (John 3:16; compare D&C 34:3).

Though it is true that we approach the Father directly in prayer, that we are entitled to "come boldly unto the throne of grace" (Hebrews 4:16), our access to Elohim is made available through Christ's mediation and intervention. "Thou didst hear me," Zenos prayed, "because of mine afflictions and my sincerity; and it is because of thy Son that thou has been thus merciful unto me, therefore I will cry unto thee in all mine afflictions, for in thee is my joy; for thou hast turned thy judgments away from me because of thy Son" (Alma 33:11). Notice in Paul's epistle to the Romans (chapter 5) that it is *through Christ*, meaning by means of his atoning sacrifice, that we are saved from death and sin:

"We have peace with God through our Lord Jesus Christ" (v. 1).

"While we were yet sinners, Christ died for us" (v. 8).

"Being now justified by his blood, we shall be saved from wrath through him" (v. 9).

"When we were enemies, we were reconciled to God by the death of his Son" (v. 10).

"We also joy in God through our Lord Jesus Christ, by whom we have now received the atonement" (v. 11).

"As by the offense of one [Adam] judgment came upon all men to condemnation; even so by the righteousness of one [Jesus Christ] the free gift came upon all men unto justification of life" (v. 18).

"That as sin hath reigned unto death, even so might grace reign through righteousness unto eternal life by Jesus Christ our Lord" (v. 21).

Under Christ

A theological battle has raged for decades in the Protestant world concerning the place of Jesus Christ in individual lives. It is known as the "Lordship controversy." Many Protestant theologians contend that when individuals receive Jesus as their personal Savior—when they are touched by the Spirit and feel to acknowledge him as Messiah—it is not necessary (at that time) to acknowledge him as Lord or Master. That is, they believe it is necessary to accept Christ (as Savior) without then turning their lives over to him (as Lord). There follows logically from this line of reasoning the idea that though these people have been "saved" through accepting Jesus in their hearts, it may be some time before they are ready to accept him as Lord and then (having developed the necessary spiritual strength in the interim) have their lives reflect the life of the Sinless One. Some even speak of accepting Jesus and then living in the category of "carnal Christians" until they are prepared to allow Jesus to govern their lives.

Latter-day Saints know and testify that to come unto Christ is to accept him willingly as Lord and Master. It is to turn our lives over to him, to submit unconditionally to his Lordship and to adopt without reservation his omniscient will. We know and we testify that in Christ is the power to transform our carnality into spirituality, to change the corruptible into incorruption, to renovate and renew the human personality. For us, to accept the Holy One as Savior is to accept him as Lord and Master.

In Christ is reconciled the irreconcilable. In him, for example, we achieve ultimate human freedom at the price of unconditional personal surrender. To surrender unconditionally to the will of a mortal may be foolhardy. We dare not allow ourselves to be at the mercy of a tyrant. But we do well to bow reverently beneath the sceptre of Christ's authority. In so doing, we find the key to personal joy and fulfillment. "I am free," Elder Boyd K. Packer explained, "and I am very jealous of my independence. . . . Choice among my freedoms is my choice to be obedient. I obey because I want to: I choose to." He continued:

> Some people are always suspicious that one is only obedient because he is compelled to be. They indict themselves with the very thought that one is only obedient because he is compelled to be. They feel that one would obey only through compulsion. They speak for themselves. I am *free* to be obedient, and I decided that—all by myself. I pondered on it; I reasoned it; I even experimented a little. I learned some sad lessons from disobedience. Then I tested it in the great laboratory of spiritual inquiry—the most sophisticated, accurate, and refined test that we can make of any principle. So I am not hesitant to say that I want to be obedient to the principles of the gospel. *I want to.* I have decided that. My volition, my agency, has been turned in that direction. The Lord knows that. . . .
>
> Obedience to God can be the very highest expression of independence. Just think of giving to Him the one thing, the one gift, that He would never take. Think of giving Him that one thing that He would never wrest from you. . . .
>
> Obedience—that which God will never take by force— He will accept when freely given. And He will then return to you freedom that you can hardly dream of—the freedom to feel and to know, the freedom to do, and the freedom to *be*, at least a thousandfold more than we offer Him. Strangely enough, the key to freedom is obedience. (*"That All May Be Edified,"* pp. 255–56.)

To be *under Christ*, under his Lordship, his leadership, under his governance, is to be yoked to Christ. "Come unto me," the Savior implores, "all ye that labour and are heavy laden, and I will give you rest. Take my yoke upon you, and learn of me; for I am meek and lowly in heart: and ye shall find rest unto your souls. For my yoke is easy, and my burden is light." (Matthew 11:28–30.) Success and happiness in this life will derive largely from our attitude toward the yoke of Christ. If we insist that we have a better idea, if we contend that we can handle all situations ourselves, if we choose alternate paths and convenient detours, then the yoke of Christ will become a coarse collar, a confining chain. If, however, we submit to Christ, "offer [our] whole souls as an offering unto him" (Omni 1:26), and yield to the enticings and promptings of his Holy Spirit, then we shall come to glory in the freedom, rejoice in the liberty, that comes in and through his love and mercies and condescensions.

President Brigham Young explained that "they who try to serve God and still cling to the spirit of the world, have got on two yokes—the yoke of Jesus and the yoke of the devil, and they will have plenty to do. They will have a warfare inside and outside, and the labor will be very galling, for they are directly in opposition one to the other. Cast off the yoke of the enemy, and put on the yoke of Christ, and you will say that his yoke is easy and his burden is light. This I know by experience." (*Journal of Discourses* 16:123.) Such a step is not, as many have supposed, an abnegation of personal freedom, but rather the beginning of dynamic individualism, the path to true freedom (see John 8:32). This is not a mindless act of blind obedience. "To bring our minds under Christ's yoke is not to deny our rationality but to submit to his revelation" (John Stott, *Life in Christ*, p. 53).

In Christ

Those who come out of the world into the true Church do so by baptism and through the laying on of hands for the reception of the Holy Ghost. The Holy Ghost is a sanctifier; his role is to cleanse dross and sin out of one's soul as though by fire. The Holy Ghost is also a revelator; his role is to make known to us the things of God. By means of the Holy Ghost we come to have "the mind of Christ" (1 Corinthians 2:16)—we come to think and feel and act as he does. To be *in Christ* is to be united to Christ, to enjoy the influence of his Spirit in our lives. Truly, as the Apostle Paul taught, "he that is joined unto the Lord is one spirit" (1 Corinthians 6:17).

It is easy to understand how it is that through his Spirit Christ can be *in us*. But the scriptures repeatedly affirm that when the revelator who is the Holy Ghost is functioning in our lives the Lord is in us and we are in him. This is a divine relationship expressing oneness and singularity of purpose. "And the Father and I are one," the Savior declared in a modern revelation. "I am in the Father and the Father in me; and inasmuch as ye have received me, ye are in me and I in you." (D&C 50:43.) Thus it is that the ancient Apostles and prophets—particularly the Apostle Paul—called upon the Saints to rid themselves of the trappings of this world, come unto Christ, be in Christ. Thus it is that the phrase "in Christ" or its cognate expressions such as "in the Lord" or "in him" occurs some 164 times in Paul's epistles to the former-day Saints.

A familiar scripture whose meaning reaches well beyond the promise of bodily resurrection is: "For since by man came death, by man came also the resurrection of the dead. For as in Adam all die, even so in Christ shall all be made alive." (1 Corinthians 15:21–22.) Men and women who follow Christ rest secure in the hope of the inseparable union of body and spirit; they also know that in Christ they may be raised from a spiritually stillborn status to a condition of life and light. They are quickened, made alive, by the power of the Holy Ghost. To the Galatians Paul penned the following: "For as many of you as have been baptized into Christ have put on Christ. There is neither Jew nor Greek, there is neither bond nor free, there is neither male nor female: for ye are all one in Christ Jesus." (Galatians 3:27–28.)

For Paul, nothing was more important than being "in

Christ." "What things were gain to me," he affirmed, "those I counted loss for Christ. Yea doubtless, and I count all things but loss for the excellency of the knowledge of Christ Jesus my Lord: for whom I have suffered the loss of all things, and do count them but dung, *that I may win Christ, and be found in him,* not having mine own righteousness, which is of the law, but that which is through the faith of Christ, the righteousness which is of God by faith." (Philippians 3:7–9, emphasis added.) Through the atoning sacrifice of Jesus Christ we are able to put off the natural man and put on Christ; in so doing we are born again unto a new life in Christ. "Therefore if any man be in Christ, he is a new creature: old things are passed away; behold, all things are become new" (2 Corinthians 5:17).

Like Christ

Jesus Christ is not only our Savior and Redeemer but also our Model, our Example. Christians seek to be like Christ, to live as he lived. His perfect obedience, his constancy and unwearied commitment to duty, and his complete submission to the will of his Father—these are the kinds of things he did that those who aspire to his glory are expected to do also.

In section 93 of the Doctrine and Covenants is to be found a marvelous pattern for the Saints, a description of how Christ developed in line-upon-line fashion to the point where he received a fulness of the Father. It might well be called "Christ's pathway to Fulness." It reads: "I, John, saw that he [Christ] received not of the fulness [of the glory of his Father] at the first, but received grace for grace; and he received not of the fulness at first, but continued from grace to grace, until he received a fulness." To receive "grace for grace" is to receive grace or divine assistance of the Father as we give of ourselves or provide divine assistance to others. To grow "from grace to grace" implies a developmental process, a progression from one level of spiritual attainment to a higher.

The modern revelation continues: "I give unto you these sayings [concerning how Christ received grace for grace and grew from grace to grace] *that you may understand and know how to worship, and know what you worship,* that you may come unto the Father in my name, and in due time receive of his fulness. For if you keep my commandments you shall receive of his fulness, and be glorified in me as I am in the Father; therefore, I say unto you, you shall receive grace for grace." (D&C 93:12–13, 19–20, emphasis added.)

We worship God our Father as did our Master, namely by serving our fellowmen and by growing line upon line to the point at which we are prepared and fit to dwell with the Father of lights. Thus perfect worship is emulation; imitation. It might thus be said that the Christian quest consists of a life devoted to the imitation of Christ. To strive with all our might to become more like him "marks the difference between the mere admiration of Him and the greater adoration of Him, between verbal veneration and genuine emulation." (Neal A. Maxwell, *Even As I Am,* pp. 35–36.)

We do all we can to pattern our lives after the only perfect life. We bend and we stretch and we push and we pull to make our will conform to his. We exert all the self-discipline and generate all the energy we can to do our duties in the home and in the Church. And we battle constantly against sin and vice and evil; we labor without ceasing to keep our thoughts and our actions clean and pure in an impure world. We are expected to do all these things, to do our part, to use all the skill and strength within our capacity to become a Christian. But we do not travel along the pathway of life very long before we realize that in the ultimate sense it is the Lord Jesus Christ who will make us like the Lord Jesus Christ. And he will do it through the cleansing and filling powers of his Holy Spirit. Again, we must do all we can do, but it is through the intervention of divine powers upon our mind and heart that we will in time become as Christ is.

The gifts and fruit of the Spirit are bestowed upon the true followers of Jesus Christ, not just as a reward for faithfulness but as a means of cleansing and perfecting their natures. This seems to be what Mormon had in mind when he spoke concerning the purifying power of charity: "Wherefore, my beloved brethren," he explained, "pray unto the Father with all the energy of heart, that ye may be filled with this love, which he hath bestowed upon all who are true followers of his Son, Jesus Christ; that ye may become the sons of God; that when he shall appear we shall be like him, for we shall see him as he is; that we may have this hope; that we may be purified even as he is pure" (Moroni 7:48).

President George Q. Cannon stated:

> I feel to bear testimony to you, my brethren and sisters, that God is the same to-day as He was yesterday; that God is willing to bestow these gifts upon His children. . . . If any of us are imperfect, it is our duty to pray for the gift that will make us perfect. Have I imperfections? I am full of them. What is my duty? To pray to God to give me the gifts that will correct these imperfections. If I am an angry man, it is my duty to pray for charity, which suffereth long and is kind. Am I an envious man? It is my duty to seek for charity, which envieth not. So with all the gifts of the Gospel. They are intended for this purpose. No man ought to say, "Oh, I cannot help this; it is my nature." He is not justified in it, for the reason that God has promised to give strength to correct these things, and to give gifts that will eradicate them. If a man lack wisdom, it is his duty to ask God for wisdom. The same with everything else. That is the design of God concerning His Church. He wants His Saints to be perfected in the truth. For this purpose He gives these gifts, and bestows them upon those who seek after them, in order that they may be a perfect people upon the face of the

earth, notwithstanding their many weaknesses, because God has promised to give the gifts that are necessary for their perfection. (*Millennial Star*, 23 April 1894, pp. 260–61.)

A Final Testimony

God has restored through Joseph Smith a system of salvation that allows all men and women to enter the realm of divine experience and partake for themselves of the powers of godliness. The fulness of the everlasting gospel has been restored to earth "that every man might speak in the name of God the Lord, even the Savior of the world" (D&C 1:20). Because of what has been made known through Joseph Smith and his successors; because of the revelations, translations, and divine oracles that have been delivered by the ministry of angels, by the voice of God, and by the power of the Holy Ghost; and because of the fact that the Holy Spirit of God has spoken plainly and unmistakably to my soul—because of these things I can testify

— that Jesus Christ is the Son of the Living God;
— that he lived, that he suffered and bled for our sins, and that he died an ignominious death on the cruel cross of Calvary;
— that he rose three days later from the tomb as a resurrected and immortal being, and that as a result of his rise from death all men and women shall likewise come forth from the dead in immortality;
— that the resurrected Jesus appeared, with his glorified and exalted Father, to the boy prophet, Joseph Smith, in the spring of 1820;
— that Joseph Smith, as a dispensation head, is the preeminent revealer of Christ to this age and generation;

— that The Church of Jesus Christ of Latter-day Saints is the only true and living Church on earth today, that it is Christ's church, and that it teaches his gospel, administers his ordinances, and is led and directed by him;

— that the Apostles and prophets who direct the Church's destiny are called and empowered and led in their sacred labors by the Lord himself;

— that Jesus Christ will come again to earth to reign as King of kings and Lord of lords, to direct his millennial church and kingdom.

These things I know. I know them as I know that I live. My prayer for each of us is that we will be true to that Lord we worship; that we will strive to be who and what we have been called to be; that we will lead and love and live as our Master has shown us; that we will be loyal to the Lord's church and his anointed servants; and that we will rely upon and trust in the mercy and grace of the Holy Messiah—all to the end that we might merit the approval of him who guides this work, and that thereby we might have peace and happiness in this world and eternal reward and glory in the world to come.

Bibliography

Benson, Ezra Taft. *The Teachings of Ezra Taft Benson*. Salt Lake City: Bookcraft, 1988.

———. *A Witness and a Warning*. Salt Lake City: Deseret Book Co., 1988.

Bonhoeffer, Dietrich. *The Cost of Discipleship*. New York: Macmillan Publishing Co., Inc., 1976.

Brown, Hugh B. *Vision and Valor*. Salt Lake City: Bookcraft, 1971.

Cannon, George Q. *Gospel Truth*. Salt Lake City: Deseret Book Co., 1987.

Clarke, Adam. *Adam Clarke's Commentary on the Bible*. Abr. Ralph Earle. Grand Rapids, Michigan: Baker Book House, 1967.

Conference Report. Salt Lake City: The Church of Jesus Christ of Latter-day Saints, October 1968; April 1971; October 1972; April 1973; October 1973; April 1975; April 1977; October 1981; April 1985; April 1986; October 1987; April 1988; April 1992; April 1993.

Crabb, Larry. *Inside Out*. Colorado Springs, Colorado: Navpress, 1988.

Dummelow, J. R., ed. *A Commentary on the Holy Bible*. New York, Macmillan Publishing Co., 1973.

Durant, Will and Ariel. *The Lessons of History*. New York: Simon and Schuster, 1968.

Evans, Richard L. *Richard Evans' Quote Book*. Salt Lake City: Publisher's Press, 1971.

George, Bob. *Classic Christianity*. Eugene, Oregon: Harvest House Publishers, Inc., 1989.

Hafen, Bruce C. *The Broken Heart*. Salt Lake City: Deseret Book Co., 1989.

Hinckley, Gordon B. *Faith, the Essence of True Religion*. Salt Lake City: Deseret Book Co., 1989.

———. *The Loneliness of Leadership*. Brigham Young University Speeches of the Year. Provo, 4 November 1969.

———. "Of You It Is Required to Forgive." *Ensign*, June 1991.

Holland, Jeffrey R. *However Long and Hard the Road*. Salt Lake City: Deseret Book Co., 1985.

Hunter, Howard W. "Jesus, the Very Thought of Thee." *Ensign*, May 1993; also found in April 1993 Conference Report.

Hybels, Bill, and Rob Wilkins. *Descending into Greatness*. Grand Rapids, Michigan: Zondervan Publishing House, 1993.

Hymns of The Church of Jesus Christ of Latter-day Saints. Salt Lake City: The Corporation of the President of The Church of Jesus Christ of Latter-day Saints, 1985.

Jessee, Dean C., ed. *The Personal Writings of Joseph Smith*. Salt Lake City: Deseret Book Co., 1984.

Journal of Discourses. 26 vols. Liverpool, England: F. D. Richards & Sons, 1851–86.

Kelly, James. "We're Not Going to Make It." *Time*, 25 January 1982.

Kimball, Spencer W. "Jesus: The Perfect Leader." *Ensign*, August 1979.

———. "Hold Fast to the Iron Rod." *Ensign*, November 1978.

Lectures on Faith. Salt Lake City: Deseret Book Co., 1985.

Lee, Harold B. "Leading As the Savior Led." *New Era*, June 1977.

Lewis, C. S. *Mere Christianity*. New York: Macmillan Publishing Company, 1952.

———. *The Weight of Glory*. Grand Rapids, Michigan: William B. Eerdmans Publishing Co., 1949.

MacArthur, John F., Jr. *Faith Works: The Gospel According to the Apostles*. Dallas, Texas: Word Publishing, 1993.

Malik, Charles H. Forum address, *BYU Studies*, vol. 16, no. 4, Summer 1976.

———. "Leadership." *New Era*, June 1977.

Maxwell, Neal A. *Even As I Am*. Salt Lake City: Deseret Book Co., 1982.

McConkie, Bruce R. "This Generation Shall Have My Word Through You." *Hearken, O Ye People*. Sandy, Utah: Randall Book Co., 1984.

———. *The Promised Messiah*. Salt Lake City: Deseret Book Co., 1978.

Millennial Star. Liverpool: The Church of Jesus Christ of Latter-day Saints, 1840–1970.

Millet, Robert L. *By Grace Are We Saved*. Salt Lake City: Bookcraft, 1989.

———. *Life in Christ*. Salt Lake City: Bookcraft, 1990.

Monson, Thomas S. "Invitation to Exaltation." *Ensign*, June 1993.

Oaks, Dallin H. "Our Strengths Can Become Our Downfall." *Brigham Young University 1991–92 Devotional and Fireside Speeches*. Provo, Utah: University Publications, 1992.

———. *The Lord's Way*. Salt Lake City: Deseret Book Co., 1991.

Pace, Glenn L. *Spiritual Plateaus*. Salt Lake City: Deseret Book Co., 1991.

Packer, Boyd K. *Let Not Your Heart Be Troubled*. Salt Lake City: Bookcraft, 1991.

———. *"That All May Be Edified."* Salt Lake City: Bookcraft, 1982.

Richards, Lawrence O. *Expository Dictionary of Bible Words*. Grand Rapids, Michigan: Zondervan Publishing House, 1985.

Richards, Stephen L. *Where Is Wisdom?* Salt Lake City: Deseret Book Co., 1955.

Rosenblatt, Roger. "The Man in the Water." *Time*, 25 January 1982.

Schlesinger, Arthur M., Jr. *The Disuniting of America*. New York: W. W. Norton & Co., 1992.

Smith, Joseph. *Teachings of the Prophet Joseph Smith*. Comp. Joseph Fielding Smith. Salt Lake City: Deseret Book Co., 1976.

Smith, Joseph F. *Gospel Doctrine*. Salt Lake City: Deseret Book Co., 1971.

Stanley, Charles. *The Wonderful Spirit-Filled Life*. Nashville: Thomas Nelson Publishers, 1992.

Stott, John. *Life in Christ*. Wheaton, Illinois: Tyndale House Publishers, Inc., 1991.

Tanner, N. Eldon. "Leading As the Savior Led." *New Era*, June 1977.

Scripture Index

BOOK OF MORMON

DOCTRINE AND COVENANTS

PEARL OF GREAT PRICE

Subject Index